A

From the modest beginnings of a pub show, the Raving Beauties' work expanded to include TV specials, national and international tours of their stage shows and poetry readings, and three collections of poetry for The Women's Press.

Their strongest contribution and acknowledgement of women has been through their books. *Bust Up!* continues this tradition in which they have pride and gratitude.

About Frances Viner

Fan Viner has spent most of her professional life in the theatre as director and actor. She writes for television and film. As well as working for pleasure she also sails and makes pottery.

About Anna Carteret

Anna Carteret's theatre work includes many years of playing leads at the Royal National Theatre, culminating with the tour of Alan Bennett's *Single Spies*.

Her London appearances began with *Big Bad Mouse*, starring Jimmy Edwards and Eric Sykes; later followed by 'Nora' in *The Doll's House*; a psychiatrist called 'Julia' in *Deceptions* by Paul Wheeler; and George Cole's wife, mistress, agent, and a member of the Royal Family in Peter Nichol's *A Piece of my Mind*.

During a recent tour of the RSC production of *Les Liaisons Dangereuses*, in which she played 'La Marquise de Merteuil', she directed the younger members of the company in Howard Brenton's *Bloody Poetry*, which played several venues, ending up at The Young Vic.

On the screen, she is probably best known for her portrayal of 'Inspector Kate Longton' in the BBC series *Juliet Bravo*, but since then she has starred in *The Shell Seekers*, *The Heat of the Day* and *Ashenden*.

Anna's love of poetry initially led her to become a founder member of the Raving Beauties. She is proud to have taken part in their productions *In the Pink*, *Make It Work* and *Tea at the Ritz*, and to have contributed to their three anthologies of women's poetry.

About Sue Jones-Davies

Sue Jones-Davies is an actor, singer and teacher. She is one half of the due Cusan Tân whose debut CD came out in April 1992. She also makes time to sail, ski, walk, read poetry and slob around.

About Dee Orr

Dee Orr has acted in most of the Raving Beauties' productions and is probably best-remembered for her spoon-playing waitress in *Tea at the Ritz*.

She began her career as a singer/percussionist before turning to acting and some of her recent television work includes a Screen Two play *The Grass Arena*, and Alan Bleasdale's award-winning *GBH*.

Dee lives in London with her two adorable cats, Sophia and Lena.

**Also by the Raving Beauties from
The Women's Press:**

In The Pink (1983)
No Holds Barred (1985)
*Fat Like The Sun: The Raving Beauties
Introduce Poems by Anna Swir* (1986)

Acknowledgements

Bust Up! would not have been possible without the generosity of all the women who wrote to us. Their commitment to themselves and to being the authors of their own lives has enabled them to give these inspiring stories to others. This book is dedicated to them and their journeys.

We would also like to thank Frederique Cassasscus, Karen Evans, Molly the python, Alison Blake Designs and especially Kate Brooks whose work and support at the inception of this book were invaluable.

BUST UP!

*The Raving
Beauties on
Surviving
Separation
and Divorce*

The Raving Beauties logo by Lucy Morahan

First published by The Women's Press Ltd, 1992
A member of the Namara Group
34 Great Sutton Street, London EC1V ODX

British Library Cataloguing in Publication Data
Bust Up!: "Raving Beauties" on Separation
and Divorce
  I. Raving Beauties
  828

ISBN 0 7043 4325 8

Typeset by Falcon Typographic Art Ltd, Fife, Scotland
Printed and bound in Great Britain by
BPCC Hazells Ltd.
Member of BPCC Ltd.

CONTENTS

Preface   xi

Women after marriage: symptoms of something *Clare*
    Venables   1

Each man kills the thing he loves *Alex Carter*   5

A long conversation *Julia Darling*   11

A bitter and painful business *Moira Dennison*   13

Standing more solidly *Andrea Perry*   19

Pick of the jumble *Linda Gould*   30

Erosion *Katie Campbell*   38

A new sense of independence *Belona Rix*   39

Owning your life *Cathy Symmonds*   43

From Here to There *Janet Craze*   49

Love letter to my son *Clare Venables*   53

Letting her go *Za*   54

Loneliness *Sun Sun Lwin*   62

Lot's wife *Roz Cowman*   65

Regaining control and self-respect *Elaine Benson*   67

Wintergarden *Agnes Maria Burns*   75

A victim no more *Frances Storey*   76

Evensong *Sun Sun Lwin*   85

funny how it all turned out *Jane Cornwell*   87

Let us leave them believing *Katie Campbell*   96

Separate lives *Margot Francis*   97

Chaos theory *Diana Barber*   107

Leave my chickens alone *Sue Thomas*   108

Prelude *Clare Venables*   118

A richer and more varied life *Margaret Edmonds*   120

PREFACE

Fan:

When the Raving Beauties edited their first book of poetry for The Women's Press, I imagine I felt in control of my life. I said in the preface that I had a lot to be grateful for. I suppose I had. I had a family, work many would find enviable and I was a feminist who could carry some of the issues she cared about into a paying public arena. But the truth of it was that I was emotionally subjugated, timid and inauthentic. Although I was challenging others to confront their compromises it came as a deep shock to realise how steadfastly I had refused to look at my own. Exhaustion and misery finally broke the spell and my partner and I agreed to a trial separation. I saw that for him this would mean a trial of every freedom known to the single man. We had tried to separate before. This time it stuck. We remained 'friends' until he found someone else.

Although I could never have found much pleasure in life within it, my attachment had been deep and primitive. Love and hate had become the same thing. I was addicted to an intensity of feeling, any feeling. I created dramas and crises in order to feel SOMETHING. I grew up in an emotional vacuum and had worked myself into a frenzy to get a feeling response from my parents. I am in no doubt that I chose my ex because of his likeness to my dad. He had the same film-star good looks and impenetrable soul. It might work out in Mills and Boon but it was useless to the child I was and, to a degree, still am.

During my relationship I had neglected my work and lost touch with my creative drive. I allowed myself to become economically dependent. Even my love for my children was hampered in its expression. One brings all of one's vitality to a great love and I felt that so much of me had been weighed and found wanting that I wasn't able to immerse myself as playfully and joyfully in loving my children as I would have wished, let alone share this with their father. This is my one deep regret, the loss of this time with my children.

My major task since separating has been to recognise myself as loveable and not to be afraid to set my standards in accordance with that fundamental belief and right. I have accomplished things in the last couple of years that have repaired my belief in myself as a unique human being with a contribution to make. As well as sharing fun and pleasure, I articulate my pain, when it arises, in order to be whole and healthy. I am a writer and feel I have finally found a professional and creative identity which suits my temperament.

In editing this book I have experienced myself as part of some larger movement. *Bust Up!* is yet another testimony to the psychological transformation of women. It is clear that many of us are making positive choices to live alone, that is, outside the 'marital' commitments which society has previously defined, endorsed and validated. The knowledge of self which fulfilling this challenge demands has the potential to have much wider effects on all our lives on earth.

Sue:

We were going to be your average family unit, nothing special, but secure – pets, holidays, growing closer together as the years went by. I don't think we ever got to first post. When I was pregnant with our fourth child my partner left and everything came apart at the seams.

I never expected to see light at the end of the tunnel. I didn't see how there could be. The trauma of losing my partner was compounded by his behaviour after he had gone and the fact that our third child had been stillborn. I was in a black hole where nothing was as it seemed. None of my past values and beliefs applied. I doubted for my sanity. In retrospect I think the emotional trauma of losing Rebecca went on hold and didn't come out until years later. Somehow, at the time, you keep going.

It is now six years later. Recovery has been slow and comprised many factors. The first important step was to go back to my childhood home of Wales. That was a gut decision. It felt absolutely right, even though the practicalities of it were difficult. I trusted myself – and that was the most difficult and the most precious thing I could have done. I was honouring myself in the face of criticism, misunderstanding, and strong emotional pressures. Not honouring yourself is the greatest act of betrayal you can commit. It is most often committed in the name of service to others but it leads, in varying degrees, to self-destruction.

It was a difficult first year alone. The house was cold and damp. My youngest lived with my parents while I did a teacher training course and I missed him terribly. I took out my anger and frustration on my two other children, often cruelly and unfairly. A poem by Alta sums it up:

> & all those years nobody loved me
> except her & I screamed at her & spanked
> her
> & threw her on the bed & slammed the
> door when
> i was angry & desperate for her
> father's love,
> & I cant undo all those times i frightened her

> & she loved me, she still loves me,
> i cant undo needing &
> being tortured with loneliness
> until I cried out at her,
> who loved me even in my needy loneliness.

I can't make up for that time. All I can do is make today as good as possible.

Eventually, I began to experience moments of calm. I began to allow myself to acknowledge how much I loved the countryside; the rain on the hills and trees – not as some romantic fantasy but as a source of deep-rooted strength and harmony. It was the first step on my road to recovery.

I try, now, to live one day at a time. I'm not in contact with my ex-partner. I tried every possible way of not cutting him off totally, but it made me too unhappy. A year ago I decided I didn't want any communication with him. Access arrangements are made through a friend. Just for today, it's the right decision.

My maintenance is good, compared to other single parents. But the boys and I are still at a much reduced level of income. I've yet to meet a woman with children who was better off financially after separation. I supplement our income as a self-employed actress/singer. The job prospects are precarious, the money variable, the hours completely unsociable, and I love it. It's a selfish choice but if I didn't feed that side of me I couldn't handle the rest.

My parents have supported me steadfastly, financially, practically and emotionally. The state does not support women, so our essential back-up systems are always family or friends.

I'm a healthier woman today. I have moments of despair and depression, but they are exceptions. It is difficult to get worked up over things that used to loom large, housework, imaged slights, missed job opportunities. I've left perfectionism miles behind. I'm having a go at whatever takes my fancy – tennis, skiing, sailing. It's wonderful.

I love my three sons very much. I want them to have healthy lives, healthy relationships. I don't want them to make the mistake I – and so many others – make – of looking for qualities in a partner they need to develop in themselves. Women are encouraged to see men as responsible for financial stability and social position, while men look to women to provide an emotional and spiritual centre. I want my sons to be responsible for themselves. To believe that 'when you look in a mirror you're looking at the one person who can make you happy'.

I'm still on my own and I like it like that. It's taken me so long to get well, that I'm in no rush to change things. I don't rule out the possibility of a relationship but it would have to be one that would enhance my life not diminish it. There don't seem to be many of those around.

I still have to be vigilant about my well-being. I have to struggle not to compare myself with others, which leaves me either bitter and frustrated or smug and superior. I have come to recognise that such comparisons are a symptom of a loss of my own sense of uniqueness; and that I should use all my energy in the fulfilment of me.

My favourite quotation sums up my philosophy to healthy living and, by extension, to healthy relationships and ultimately deep fearless love – 'You do not need to be loved, not at the cost of yourself. Of all the people you will meet in a lifetime, you are the only one you will never leave or lose.'

Anna:

Society is only just breaking free of the notion that women are destined for marriage. Our conditioning instils guilt in those of us who put a career first, or who, for their own reasons, prefer to live alone or with another woman. In fact many women are still encouraged to subject their lives and aspirations to those of their husbands', which means sacrificing their independence in order to devote themselves entirely to his needs and desires.

To me, that very narrowing down of woman's hopes and ambitions is one of the principal causes of the various disabilities, economic and otherwise, under which she labours today.

Marriage or its equivalent, is probably the toughest challenge we ever tackle – and yet we are not educated to prepare us for what it entails. It is surprising, given the ideals and expectations fed to us by the media, together with insidious pressure from the family, that any relationship can withstand the strain, particularly when there are children to protect. It is unreal to expect one individual to replace all that a woman has sacrificed to become a couple, let alone to fulfil the ideals she had been led to expect. This disappointment can lead to disillusionment with the relationship – and eventually a breakdown of communication.

The change in moral attitudes towards separation, and the loss of the social stigma of divorce, has not lessened the pain of the actual experience for everyone concerned – but what is encouraging is that it can now be a very positive process in the end. Through the experiences of the women in this book, we can share their journey of self-exploration, growth, and reawakening as individuals – their courage in taking on the responsibilities of a home, children and a job simultaneously. This is often achieved with the support of women friends who can prove crucial at a time of such vulnerability.

Is it necessary to go through this baptism of fire to achieve the courage, strength, self-knowledge they have found? Could they have acquired it within the context of a relationship? Or does what most people regard a 'marriage' or 'partnership' automatically place strictures on people's freedom, ability to take responsibility, change direction or 'grow'?

Most of us, when we undertake these commitments, are either too young or too inexperienced to know what it is we really want from the relationship. And, in many cases, the women matures through the experience, and changes from a willing innocent into a questioning, more demanding equal – and it can be difficult for the man to adjust without feeling threatened. Yet the very process of growth necessitates change – to which, for some reason, human nature is resistant.

The economic climate has influenced the status of the sexes in a relationship – when men are made redundant, for example, women are forced to become bread-winners. So women have the opportunity to enjoy the experience of getting out into the world, while men have a taste of being housebound. This can create friction if it continues – or alternatively open eyes to the needs of partners.

Ideally, an equal, fulfilling partnership should involve finding out one's own priorities and limits and those of one's partner and then working towards achieving a balance. This should enable each to help the other grow, while retaining the freedom to be themselves within the relationship.

But ironically, I suspect that this takes the very courage and independence of spirit learnt through the experience of separation.

Dee:

'Till death us do part.' Well, how do you mourn a love that has died? With great difficulty, a lot of courage, support from friends and loved ones – and by keeping your sense of humour.

Being involved with the life of this book had made me realise that, as women, we are not alone in our struggle to survive. How far do we go before saying 'no more'? When things are bad, why do we stay? In a fearful, masochistic way, we do it for the children; we do it because we are afraid to be left on our own; we do it because we are sometimes in fear for our lives; we do it because it's a lot easier than having to face ourselves each day.

Man may fight his wars to destroy, and gain, through greed, his ownership rights – but woman fights her wars to give life and nurture the very essence of being, The women within this book are part of our hope for the future – they all said 'no more'. I was amazed at their honesty, courage, strength and ability, at times, to see the funny side.

In helping to compile this book I recognised many of my own stumbling blocks. I feel that in each story there is something common to us all – something we can all identify with at some time in our lives.

I have learned a lot from this book. I hope you will too.

WOMEN AFTER MARRIAGE:
SYMPTOMS OF SOMETHING

Clare Venables

The following is a short paper describing the symptoms of women with child or children, separated, after a long marriage, from the spouse.

DETAILS OF STUDY METHOD
Numbers of women studied: One
Class of women studied: Middle
Identity of women studied: Self
Method of study: Long thinks at four o'clock in the morning

SYMPTOMS AND THOUGHT PATTERNS IMMEDIATELY AFTER BREAKDOWN OF MARRIAGE AND FOR THE FOLLOWING PERIOD OF A FEW YEARS

1. *Confusion*: 'How did that happen? How odd, I thought it was till death do us part. What happened to the Start Rite advert that we started out in? Did I mean this?'

2. *Exhilaration*: 'This is like being a student again! I'm not responsible for him! Anything is possible! I can be whoever I want to be! Crumbs! Let's spend money, let's buy clothes! Let's EAT, DRINK! Hello, world!'

3. *Night terror*: 'Will I ever speak to an adult again? It's so QUIET. How can ONE person do all this? What will happen

if I get ill? I'll die and no-one will know and they'll starve in their cots thinking I've abandoned them. Everyone knows it's just me and the babies – I'll be attacked, raped, tortured! Oh, Christ! I can't live like this. I can't BE this tired and carry on. It's not POSSIBLE. I'm going to die.'

4. *Shame:* 'I've failed; there's something wrong with me; it's my hard un-feminine fault; I'm a monster; he's a nice man; anyone else would have made it work; I'm doomed to be a misfit. I'm childish, immature, stupid not to have been happy when I had the chance.'

5. *Panic:* 'I must work otherwise we'll starve; I can't work; they'll turn into junkies; I must work or I'll go mad; I can't work; they'll go mad.'

6. *Self-pity:* 'Why did this happen to me? No-one has ever loved me; I have never loved anyone; he never understood me; no-one has ever understood me; I'm so tired; she's got all that money *and* a nice man; *they* are happy – look how he puts his arm round her, takes her home; it's not fair; why didn't I get looked after? It's not fair.'

7. *Randiness:* 'If I don't sleep with someone soon I'll spontaneously combust.'

8. *Nil libido:* 'What's sex?'

9. *Fear:* 'I'm old, ugly, tired, beastly and no-one will ever like, fancy, love me again. I am alone.'

10. *Anger:* 'Marriage is impossible for women, life is impossible for women, and it's not going to get better IN MY LIFETIME. My life is finished but I have to go on as if it isn't.'

SYMPTOMS AND THOUGHT PATTERNS TEN YEARS AFTER BREAKDOWN OF MARRIAGE

1. *Love:* 'Sometimes I feel I can't keep up with all the people I love, that I haven't got enough to go round, that I must settle down and focus it all on one person. Whoops! That's what I did before, so perhaps not.'

2. *Pride:* 'I've survived. The kids have survived, even flourished in a minor way. They seem to quite like me, and their dad. They love their half-brother.'

3. *Loneliness:* 'It's dark in here, no-one can feel it except me. But it's not cold any more. I know this place. I can handle it.'

4. *Devotion:* 'To the strength of the children, to my friends, to my work, to the house, to the women who have helped me as nannies, babysitters, friends, colleagues, writers. To lovers, male friends and colleagues.'

5. *Anger:* 'It's taken so long to begin to learn how to live, that I have hardly any time left. That is because of our history, and I spent all this time, almost a lifetime, thinking that it was my fault. I didn't learn how to live *my* life in time to live my *whole* life; Oh, the waste, the waste! I can't bear it.'

6. *Compulsion:* To read every Make-Yourself-Over book ever written. (Secondary symptom: slight depression, after reading every Make-Yourself-Over book ever written, that life doesn't seem to have changed.)

7. *Sadness:* 'The kids will have their problems over coming from a split home; they will not have the automatic confidence I wanted them to have; I don't know how to make things work with my ex-husband and his second wife; I would like not to be a "divorcee".'

8. *Fear:* 'The house will fall down; I will go bankrupt; I can't cope; I am getting old with no "security".'

9. *Clarity:* 'Even if I was married, all of 8 would still apply, though I might not know it.'

10. *Occasional joy:* in the interest of life; in its mystery, horrors, patterns, randomness, unknownness, stupidity, comedy.

ANALYSIS OF SYMPTOMS

It is clear that the subject has made progress, over the ten years, from mainly negative to mainly positive symptoms. However, it would be wise to look at the second list of symptoms in the light of the fact that it is difficult for anybody to be truthful about their current life. The subject may be unconsciously repressing negative responses to her present state in order to present her life, to herself and others, as good. But it is clear that the shock of separation and having to take responsibility has made her come to terms with loneliness, and has made her find meaning in that which was originally most terrifying, i.e. her responsibility for her children, work, chaos, love, anger. She obviously now has a sense of beginning to live her own life, albeit rather late.

CONCLUSION

This woman's life is not yet over, and so it is perhaps too early to come to any conclusions; however, there are some tentative thoughts we can suggest.

It is significant that the subject does not condemn the state of marriage itself. What she does seem to suggest is that she was not able to find her own autonomy and growth within it, and she is glad that, despite the pain of separation, she was able to begin to find this autonomy. But there seems to be some residual anger that it is so difficult, particularly for women, to find this growth within the companionship of marriage. The subject seems to have begun to find a certain kind of confidence, which the Make-Yourself-Over books, to which she refers, can seem to equate with endless happiness. It is clear, from paying attention to even her positive symptoms, that endless happiness is *not* the result to be expected from making a stab at autonomy. In fact, the subject has seemed to experience quite a share of misery; but it is certain that she thinks that the misery has been both meaningful and worthwhile, and cannot be divided from the joys of the journey towards understanding.

4

EACH MAN KILLS THE THING HE LOVES

Alex Carter

In three weeks' time we will go to court. We will stand, daggers drawn, the father of my three children and I. It is almost four years since we separated; five if you include the year of death.

In that time I have touched hell, grown up through the experience and survived. I have known what it is to want to kill. (Of all the emotions, the desire to annihilate the person I once loved has been the most terrifying.) During that period, blind duty gave me stability; a small circle of friends provided equilibrium; work became an escape; reading a kind of therapy; and cuddling the children was all I could do most days to reassure them.

I lived a split life. While my emotional and material world were falling apart, part of me was growing strong beyond recognition. Day-to-day survival was my first objective. I remember sitting, head in hands, wondering if I would be able to afford soap and toothpaste! The things that had once seemed important became trivial. Shopping became streamlined as I assessed the importance of peripheral products. I was very vulnerable. Women friends, wonderfully practical and kind, listened and brought food parcels. They surreptitiously hid treats in corners for me to find after their visits. Their hugs were reassuring and their tolerance appreciated. Men offered advice and propositions!

I started to reassess everything I had taken for granted; and I started to write, which became my salvation.

The steps I took towards freedom, though tentative at first, have grown in confidence. My mother always thought herself unlucky, with that familiar, sighing resignation of many women of her generation. But I believe that luck has nothing to do with it. We are in control of our own destinies. I stopped being a victim and strove for independence. I'm not quite there, but I'm well on the way. *I have goals.*

Everything I read during the breakup of my marriage seemed to have significance. Poetry, fact or fiction – each piece held some deep message. It was as though I had awoken from a long sleep and had to learn to live again.

One article I read had a major effect. It suggested that when people split up, and think back over the years, they realise that that relationship had never been right in the first place. This observation seemed so true to me that it stopped me from blaming myself on the spot. It dawned on me that, from the start of our relationship, Tom had been powerful and very critical. I had slowly begun to acquiesce with his damning judgement and had formed a shell around myself to shield the vulnerable me from the unrelenting, subtle savagery. He had taken up where my father had left off by constantly finding fault and hardly ever being complimentary.

We had met at college. Although he was only two years older than me, his experiences were broad and mine were narrow. College life was liberation for me. I had come from a quiet family on the outskirts of an industrial town. My parents played bridge and gin rummy. I went wild when I left home! Tom had been brought up in a large family – one of seven kids. His dad had left when he was very young and his mother brought up some of her brother's children as well as all of her own.

After several disastrous relationships, I had just begun to come to terms with my independence, feeling strong and confident, when Tom and I met. He quickly cut me down to size. I was never allowed to talk about unhappiness because that was a bourgeois, middle-class concept and paled in comparison with his background. I spent most of the next fifteen years in a semi-alcoholic haze.

After Tom completed his studies, he started full-time work. And I became pregnant. He was not happy in his job, and had constant arguments with his employers – and me. He never seemed to be able to sort out his relationships with anyone. While I had babies, he started gambling and lying to me about money. And then the gambling got out of control. One Christmas when I was pregnant with number three, I got landed with a massive bookmaker's bill. I had wrapped, packed, cooked, cleaned, done the business. I had sympathised with his problems, put up with sleepless nights, tried to cajole him into a good mood, taken his criticisms about dusty corners, fat thighs. The baby had a cold. I was tired. Things were not PERFECT. I told him I couldn't cope and was going to have an abortion.

My God, how I have lived to regret that outburst! As he raised his hand to strike, I looked him straight in the eye and mentally withdrew. I folded up and packed away the nice, good, conforming me . . . for ever.

I made up my mind that if we were to stay together, we needed a new footing. For the children's sake, I did not want the marriage to end. I deluded myself that as two reasonable, adult human beings we would work something out.

The following day he packed his bags and walked out. I could not speak. I did not want to speak. It had always been me who had made conciliatory gestures, and I didn't want to do that again this time.

During the following week, a letter campaign started; and this was just the beginning of a consolidated attack which was to go on for the next three years.

Eventually he returned. I had calmed down in his absence

and I explained to him that my feelings for him had died but that if we could continue in amicable harmony on a different level we would be okay. He said that the feeling was mutual and that was fine with him. I, stupidly, breathed a sigh of relief.

Things became clearer to me. I had been drinking, regularly though not excessively. That had to stop. I wanted to see clearly.

The next twelve months were sheer hell. He was utterly miserable and said that if I no longer loved him, being married was pointless. I pleaded for time. Looking back, I know that if he had given me the space I needed we could have worked something out. I am sure that my strong sense of duty, which had always stopped me from keeling over completely, would have led me back to working at the relationship. I tried to be kind and fair, but would never be bamboozled again. Perhaps because the whole power base had changed, he could not, and would never, adjust.

I suggested marriage guidance. This was met with unbelievable anger. When I tried to discuss things with him he clammed up. I realised with slowly dawning horror that we had spent the last twelve years talking about politics and very little else.

I tried, more than anything, to protect the children from any unnecessary pain. I have always tried to be truthful with them, but did not feel they should know *too* much, although I tried to answer questions. But then he started to use them. When a friend had a party I hadn't been able to go to, she rang up to give me a full report. I relayed this to Tom and the kids and he turned to them, sneering, 'See, she'd rather be with her friends than with you!' I looked at the children's faces and knew that dramatic new rules had been introduced into the ball game.

From then on the children were used as pawns in the most despicable way. He told our daughter that he was leaving us, but that she was not to tell anyone. I only found out days later when I discovered her weeping into the night. Soon after, he wrote on the calendar that he was going, and announced it to the children one teatime, then stopped them running to me for comfort. He went on to use every emotionally vicious trick in the book to try and hurt us all. We both knew that I could cope with my own pain, but not with it being inflicted on them. I recognised that I had to get out.

He yelled and screamed but eventually he went.

The next twelve months were heaven and hell. I have had some of my best days ever, along with some of my worst.

The worst have been caused by the sheer volume of venom to which Tom has subjected us. I went to see the solicitor and clearly remember saying that Tom cared enough for his children to make reasonable arrangements. As I write this, after four years, we still do not have a settlement. Despite a court order, Tom did not pay the mortgage on the house and the building society nearly foreclosed. The only stability the children had at this time was their school and their home. I fought hard to keep it.

The best thing to come out of all the pain is that the relationships I have with friends, family and, most of all, the children have been strengthened and have brought great joy. My women friends have been unerringly supportive both emotionally and financially. They have given me the confidence to grow and become strong. My mother and I exorcised our ghosts, and a couple of close men friends have saved me from becoming bitter about the whole male species. I now value people more than anything else in the world. Nothing will ever measure up to the love and warmth which my family and friends have given me.

Through all this I started writing.

I joined a writers' group and after reading *In the Pink*

feverishly typed my first poems, some of which have been published.

Meanwhile, I got freelance work as a publisher's reader. A vacancy for an editorial assistant came up, and they gave me the job! Next year I will be employed in a full-time capacity and will be truly independent for the first time in my life. It is my goal to become my own woman. I am single-minded and determined.

Tom is back in town now. He has a new woman in his life and sees the children on a more regular basis. They are building a new and, I hope, stronger relationship. The two eldest are doing extremely well at school and the youngest is beginning to catch up after her eighteen months of inability to concentrate. I do not think their behaviour shows any gross signs of trauma. I keep in touch with the social worker who was called in by Tom to check his accusation of cruelty. She has been wonderful. My solicitor has been great, but to talk to a woman about the problems made all the difference.

I do not know what the future will bring. I do not think about it. But I do know that I *never* want to share a mortgage, bank account, insurance policy, again. If I ever give myself again, it will be on *my* terms and involve mutual respect. Maybe that doesn't exist. I don't have time to find out at the moment. I'll keep that on hold. I feel that I am now the eagle when I used to be the mouse. I will never scurry around as victim again, for now I am the hunter. Mostly . . . it feels good!

A LONG CONVERSATION

Julia Darling

first the babies . . .
remember that time they were sick
and you and I, drowning in the smell of vomit
laughed because it was so awful
it couldn't get worse

then the husbands
unlaughing unfaithful unfriendly
fuelling our mutual despair
locked in our fetid back rooms
we sent out flares
hoping the other would hear

at the mother and toddler group
we sneered and tried to get
the best biscuits, refusing
to idolise our children
we played with the pastry
and talked of mistakes

when the husbands left
we raged on each other's doorsteps
packed picnic baskets
together we made a crowd
at the park, the museum
we worked hard that year

our new definition
was not in the catalogue
we got drunk in the kitchen
knew fear, faced aloneness
and never lied
about smacking our children

it's not over
ours is a long conversation
now uncluttered with husbands
our faces seem stronger
the future much longer
all our colours are richer and deeper

A BITTER AND PAINFUL BUSINESS

Moira Dennison

It's August 1990 and I'm at the Edinburgh Fringe Festival. Not much to write about, you might think, but wait . . . I'm here on my own, on my own terms, by my own choice and enjoying my own company. Five firsts in one go!

It's taken me eleven years to get this far. I bear a slight resemblance to the me of earlier years but there is one big difference – I like myself. That's been the hardest lesson to learn. I spent so much time trying to escape from me, doing anything to stop being alone, but ultimately I caught up with myself and liked what I found.

I got married at twenty-two to a man who was a bit of a surprise to all of my friends. He was in the City and very conventional with a career mapped ahead of him which could only be enhanced by a wife and, after a suitable pause, a child. I quickly discovered that the only way I could cope with City life was by drinking and hoping that my nervousness and gaucheness would be covered up by what I presumed would be a veneer of worldly sophistication. All that happened was that I got drunk in a number of rather remarkable places – Les Ambassadeurs, The Grosvenor House Hotel, Henley . . . you get the picture. Part of the problem was that although I had a job I didn't have a career. I was working for the GLC, preparing cases for prosecution under the London Building

Acts, while my husband was dealing in Eurobonds. I don't think we even bothered with the 'what did you do at the office today?' stage. There was already too much of a gulf.

In the circumstances I did what many have done before and what thousands will do after – I got pregnant. I think I felt motherhood would focus my energies and frustrations into a positive channel and give me a break during which I could reappraise my life. This sounds so naïve now that I'm ashamed to write it down, but it's the truth or as near as I can get to it.

So, at the age of twenty-eight I became a parent. No one tells you how tiring babies are. They are exhausting and domineering and the highs in their development are matched by an extensive selection of lows when their chosen method of communication – usually a high-pitched, ear-shattering wail – will literally drive you to tears. But those exhausting days gradually faded away and I decided to get a part-time job. I ended up in the last days of the GLC's administration, co-ordinating a group based in the Piazza of Covent Garden.

Then I started examining my life and became very unhappy with what I saw. The crucial moment came during the winter, when the Ethiopian crisis was just being brought to the attention of many people in the West. I went to a ball, resplendent for the first time in my life in a taffeta gown, and spent the night quizzing bankers over their attitude to Ethiopia while the alcohol flowed freely and food designed to be picked at and discarded was piled on to our plates. Evidently I was drunk but this was a key point in my life – the point at which I realised I just couldn't play the game any more.

During all this our sex life had suffered. Babies and politics do not good bedfellows make. I was frustrated, my husband was frustrated, and the baby thought that the marital bed was the nearest thing to heaven on earth. Something had to give, and it was me. An old friend reappeared on the scene

14

– someone I had never really got over. His relationship was in the process of breaking up and we took up our glasses of Blackthorn Cider where we had left them a few years earlier. I thought that I could go out and have a few beers, see a band and walk back into my life as a mother. What I hadn't reckoned on was developing a taste for the beer and the bands. I also discovered that I liked sex – but it wasn't with my husband.

You know what's coming, don't you? I left my husband one night in high dramatic style. A note pinned to the teddy bear, a bundle of clothes for me and my son, and a car outside with its engine running for a quick getaway.

But I soon discovered that the devil you know is an absolute sweetie compared with the devil you don't. I'd a job with no prospects (abolition was looming), nowhere to live, and a child to bring up. And on top of this, I was trying to sort out my relationship with someone who was trying to sort out his relationship with someone else. It all came to pieces very soon. The people I had been staying with decided that my child and I added an extra dynamic they could do without and so we were left with no other choice but to return to the marital home with my son back in his nursery and me on the floor in the spare room.

Divorce was a bitter and painful business. I was divorced for adultery with an unknown man (known to us all) and signed a financial agreement which this year made me shake in my shoes when I tried to meet it. I packed up my bags and moved into a flat with my son. He stayed a week with me and a week with his father and I tried to live on my own for the first time in my life. I hated it. The thought of closing the door behind me at night with only a black-and-white TV for company sent shivers down my spine. I took to going out somewhere, anywhere, in an attempt to stave off the inevitable turning off of the light. I was still involved with my male friend and it was that relationship which was to dominate the next few years.

15

There were other factors in my life at that time, of course. One of them was money or, to be more exact, the complete lack of it. My salary when I first moved into my flat was around £5575. I got monthly maintenance to help meet my son's expenses but then the Inland Revenue reared its iniquitous head and decreed that maintenance was taxable income and the person who paid it was rewarded for being a good man and true by getting tax relief on it. There's nothing like hitting a woman when she's down, is there?

One month I was left with £10 after I had paid all the bills. That was the month that the damp rotted the sofa bed and ruined a large hunk of newly laid and horrendously expensive carpet. It was not a good time.

When I moved in I left part of the twentieth century behind. I didn't have a fridge, a freezer, a TV, a phone, a sofa or a proper bed. And what's more, I didn't get any of them for about three years until I remortgaged.

In between a dodgy relationship and an escalating debt crisis I had to re-think my career strategy. I'd never known what I wanted to be when I grew up and I still didn't. I moved into a secretarial admin job with a major national charity and by sheer luck was in the right place at the right time and gained some really invaluable campaigning and PR experience. But any thoughts of being a spectacular, albeit late-starting, campaigner were rapidly brought down to earth when I had to accommodate my son's needs around a career's demands.

It wasn't easy then and it isn't easy now. I have a very hectic schedule in my present job with yet another national charity, and although I've left the typewriter far behind, I'm still juggling meetings and tutorials, speaking engagements and school assemblies.

My major problem with the new man was that I thought I had a relationship whilst he didn't. I still maintain that we must have – how else could you account for the misery and anger that getting out of it cost? It suited both of us to have a

16

willing accomplice to hit the town with, and indeed the good times (a bit blurred around the edges) were exceptionally good. But oh, the bad days . . .

My friend got involved with other women. I always knew about it, and it always hurt. But I stuck it out stoically because I figured he'd come back eventually. I didn't feel that the rôle of martyr suited me so I tried to pretend that nothing was up. Occasionally I'd blow up and then my women friends would get long phonecalls to help me talk it through.

And so the days, months and years rolled on. My life was split in two – time with my friend and time with my son. It was almost as if I had two identities. I often tried to get out of the relationship. I bought the books (*Women Who Love Too Much*, etc.). I identified with the women. And then I went right on doing what I'd always been doing. I just couldn't see a way forward because I was too scared of how much it would hurt and too scared to face up to living my life for myself without another adult to focus on.

A culmination of pressures were bubbling away: my son, my career, my money worries, my mother's increasing ill health and my split existence. Then something decisive happened and I finally made the break I always knew I would have to make. Or was it made for me?

The first time I left I thought that I was leaving for something else, for someone else. The second time, I was leaving to face myself and all the things I'd dreaded and feared about being alone.

But I did it. The only way I felt I could get through was to cut myself off from him completely. If he was going somewhere, I wouldn't. It may sound childish but it worked. My good friends and true were always there when I needed them, my son was delighted that we'd parted company and my parents needed more and more of my time. I decided that crying over spilt milk wasn't going to do any good and so any time I felt myself to be getting maudlin, I remembered the bad times. That soon shook me up! There were times when I needed just to howl into the wind and feel a tad sorry for myself, but I managed to retain a sense of proportion. If I used a friend as a sounding block, I always thanked them and hopefully made them realise that they were really helping me through. The last thing I wanted was for my friends to start feeling used and abused. That was a guilt I simply couldn't face.

I started looking at my home and spending time there and liking it. I never got to the stage of cooking beautifully presented meals on a tray resplendent with napkins and a rose for my solitary evenings – it was more like lean cuisine in a bowl in front of the TV. But at least it was my TV, in my house. I read masses of books, took myself out for strolls around the neighbourhood, dusted down my exercise bike – anything to make me stay in one place for long enough to begin to like myself and my surroundings.

And that really is it. I should have done it sooner, of course. But until I was ready, until I could actually see that there was another way, I was trapped in a mess completely of my own making. Looking back, I don't really know why I was so scared: nothing is more scary than trying to live your life through other people.

STANDING MORE SOLIDLY

Andrea Perry

I'll start with the first image that comes to mind at the beginning of the real separation. It is of lying in bed at night in my studio flat, wide awake, alert to every creak, every door bang, every tiny sound on the landing and stairs outside my flat door. It is of getting out of bed, time after time, to check that the chair I have positioned between the door and wall is still securely in place. I have put it there to ensure that should he get into the flat somehow, I would at the very least have a moment of warning before he entered my room. Fear grips my throat and crushes my chest. I leave lights on – he might believe I have company; I switch lights off – he'll know I'm at home. My imagination is working overtime and panic is rising. Writing this, I can still recognise the taste of that feeling.

I met 'Rick' when I was a volunteer at a 'dry' hostel for homeless alcoholic men. Six years on I am appalled by my naïveté at that time, my inability to listen to professional warnings about not getting involved with the 'residents'. Perhaps I had convinced myself that as we had both left the hostel when we began our relationship, everything would be okay.

Rick had been an early member of the drama group I ran at the hostel. He was energetic, insightful and very good at drama improvisation when he wasn't challenging my shaky

19

leadership of the group with his witty asides. We started play-ing squash together, initially with other residents, eventually by ourselves. When he moved on to more independent living and I left to begin therapy training, we continued to meet, and after a while became lovers. There were many happy and relaxed times: his sober self was immensely creative, witty and affectionate, and he seemed very supportive and romantic. We played such a lot – squash, cards, table tennis – with words and with one another's bodies. We created a wonderful world of fantasy and fun, and both of us cherished Rick's ideas of using his experiences to help other people and to develop the art techniques he'd worked on in prison. I didn't know anything of his 'other side'. I believed that what I saw of this intuitive, brave-spirited, loving man was all of him.

I preferred it when we were by ourselves. When we met up with other people I felt I had to lie about where we'd met, about paying for him, about believing his exaggerated public claims about his future. On our own these claims seemed feasible and realistic. I guess there was excitement for well-behaved, conventional me in this blue-eyed bad lad, and I drank in his stories of terrible experiences with foster parents and children's homes, of time in prison and on the streets. I felt such empathic pain and pity for the lonely, abused little boy he'd been. He got a job as a brick layer, I got into my training and found part-time group work in a mental health day centre. Things seemed to be working out well.

One day we were invited to a Rastafarian wedding. It was a great honour, and we were thrilled to be included and fêted as friends of the groom, whom we'd met on the squash courts. It was a brilliant party. When Rick asked me how I would feel if he had a single glass of champagne, I felt very mature and told him I was not his mother. Ha! I had no idea I was already well on the way to becoming her stand-in. The inevitable and speedy passage from one glass, to several, to spirits, alarmed me; but his behaviour, initially amorous and funny, later embarrassing, loud and sentimental, wasn't so different from my own or other people's to worry me unduly. On the way home, however, and all through the night until he collapsed unconscious, it was very different. He cursed and swore at me in language I'd literally never heard, made outrageous accusations and demands, criticised me, my life and my friends with utter hatred and contempt. I was devastated and terrified. I remember crouching in a corner listening to him and not daring to take my eyes from his face, thinking this can't be happening. He sounded coherent: I think that was what was most frightening – he didn't seem drunk, as I had known 'drunk' before. All the care I felt I had extended to him, all the things I valued, were systematically being ripped apart and the worst thing was that some of what he shouted seemed true. I was too frightened to do more than crouch and listen.

In the morning I felt shattered and bewildered. He, naturally, had a terrible hangover. He cried and was extremely penitent; he promised it would never happen again. He told me I was the only person he loved, that he would prove it to me, and that if I could only love and help him enough, things would be all right. I'm ashamed to admit that I even felt smug – I, who hated conflicts and arguments, could weather a bout like this and still love him. I felt adult and mature and magnanimous. But not angry – certainly not angry.

There was peace for a while, then it happened again. And again. I told no one. Over the next few months I gradually cut contact with friends. I couldn't accept social invitations because, inevitably, there would be alcohol involved. If I asked for no alcohol to be there, there would be questions. If I said nothing, and we went, the consequences were too frightening to contemplate. So, little by little, I became engulfed in his alcoholic world. I found the vodka bottles in brown paper bags stuffed at the back of my cupboards and said nothing, feeling completely invaded and sick. I was paralysed. I was afraid to say no to him, for fear of inciting him to worse treatment of me, but I was also burying even faint flickers of outrage at his behaviour. I felt I had no right to object; I must just try harder to cope and understand. He had had such a hard life, mine was privileged by comparison. I had to be the special one who could endure and forgive all. But really, by denying my own feelings, I was colluding in the construction of a terrifying rage-monster that very nearly destroyed us both – a creation made up of both our angers.

One night I felt sufficiently embarrassed by his behaviour on the train home to say something. He stormed off and I didn't see him for a long time. Then he turned up at my house in the middle of the night, on crutches, his leg bruised and bandaged, his eyes heavy with pain and tiredness. How can you turn away someone in that state, when they say they have no one else to turn to, even when you feel a sense of dread? He lay in my small flat, apparently incapacitated, day after day while I went to work, feeling terribly frustrated. But despite his leg, he managed to get out to the pub. I never knew what to expect when I got home – abuse and accusations, burnt saucepans and singed carpets, or a display of all the cleaning he'd done and romantic overtures. It felt as though walls were closing in on us. I felt totally trapped. I still couldn't get angry with him. I felt, alternately, a victim of his aggression and responsible for rescuing him.

Then something strange began to happen. Lying in bed at night, I started to have fears that I would kill him in my sleep. I'd never had such thoughts before; it was difficult to turn my mind to something else. The only way I could get to sleep was by holding on to a crucifix I wore round my neck and praying to a God I didn't really believe in. One night I woke up suddenly and found that he was completely cold. I was terrified – I believed for an instant I'd killed him. The blanket had just slipped off, but now there was no peace, even at night.

At college I was learning about bonding, boundaries, the damaging effects of repressing feelings and ways of enabling their release. At work I was helping other women to become more self-assertive. But the pain of making the connection to my own situation was too great. I was denying that I needed help. The nights drew in; I was living on cigarettes, coffee and a growing sense of hysteria. My self-respect had completely disintegrated. Then I discovered a book with a deceptively inviting title, *Getting Them Sober*. I recognised myself immediately as being 'co-dependent' and consumed the entire contents of the book alone in a café one evening. One of the things it suggested (within an overall framework of the co-dependent working on her own problems, and not her alcoholic partner's) was that as rational conversation could not be held if he had been drinking, one should suggest discussion be held later, and then refuse to engage further.

This tactic, effective though it may be, should not be tried when you live in a studio flat with only one exit, when you are naked in bed with your drunk and angry partner with the lights turned off. I felt quite powerful for the first few moments of silent refusal to argue back at him, even smug as the volume of his demands increased. It's working, I thought – I can do it. Then he found my neck and started trying to strangle me. Now I can only remember short moments of that night: me, half-clothed and absolutely terrified, trying to work out how quickly he could move to block my exit from the flat; him, his face twisted with rage, his fist inches from my nose as he held my head and threatened to smash my face across the wall; me begging him not to. I did whatever he asked and whatever I could think of that might placate him. Eventually we slept, or rather he did.

My therapist came to my home the next night to talk to us both. I was too afraid to go home and tell him to leave myself. When he walked out, taking the keys with him, she stayed on until I could get a locksmith and move all his stuff

23

out of the flat. Then I went away to stay with friends, terrified that he might be somewhere, anywhere, watching me, about to attack. I was entirely out of contact with any anger of my own. When I got back, he was outside the front door. We went to a café and I explained that the relationship was over and that I would only meet him in public places; that I did care but that it had to end.

He didn't accept it easily. From then on I lived in fear of being alone in the flat, of some kind of retaliation if I didn't comply with his demands for meetings, for letters and phonecalls. He pushed and pushed at me for two months, trying steadfastly to break every boundary I tried to set. And then I found myself back in a situation of total helplessness – alone in an empty house with a drunk and increasingly angry Rick. I managed to get out and fled to my oldest friend, Marianne. I had told her nothing of what had happened. Now I was in complete despair. Not only had I allowed things to completely degenerate once, I was now on the verge of allowing – perhaps almost inviting – it all to happen again.

Marianne was horrified, but she was very clear. She said that I must write to Rick and break off contact immediately, saying that as I could no longer trust him, I could not be his friend. She said that until I had the self-respect to do this, then she would no longer be able to see me, because I wouldn't be the person she thought I was. I will always thank her for that. I said yes, but when I gave the letter to a friend to deliver to Rick as she insisted, I felt I was killing him, and a part of myself. One of us would die, I was sure of it. My fear and anxiety became stronger than after he had left my flat. The letters came, penitent, then angry, then vaguely threatening. Then silence, which was almost worse. I walked with my shoulders hunched and in constant fear of what I would find when I opened my front door, to go out or to come in.

Then there was the guilt. I felt I had abandoned Rick.

Leaving him felt like letting him drown. Or worse, like pushing aside a weaker swimmer in the struggle for the only available life-belt. I still had connections in the real world. I found I did have friends who I realised valued and loved me. Far from criticising, they held me and listened endlessly whilst I told and retold what had happened. But when I wasn't thinking of Rick as a knife-carrying shadow at my heels, I imagined him isolated, lonely and desperate, back on the streets. I felt responsible. I could hear friends saying I wasn't but I felt I was.

I started keeping a diary and giving myself two small tasks a day, things I didn't feel comfortable doing, but thought would be constructive. These tasks, which I noted in my diary and ticked off like a child, involved firstly, setting assertive boundaries for myself, and secondly, becoming focussed on my own development, instead of other people's problems, i.e. trying to stop advising and 'helping'. I had no problem with the taking-shoddy-shoes-back-to-the-shop form of assertiveness, but saying what I really felt in close relationships was something else. And not to give advice to friends! Or become involved with their problems! What else do you talk about? I must have looked like a fish – opening my mouth to suggest something 'helpful' and then closing it again. I felt empty and useless. It was if there was suddenly nothing to say. I felt either embarrassed and conspicuous, or left out of things and vulnerable – in no way the equal of other people. I became very aware of being in my body, surrounded by other bodies, which made me feel shy and uncomfortable, feelings I tried to avoid, with food and cigarettes. It was as if I had become my 'real self' not allowing myself to fly out of it on a stream of heady words and ideas, not really to do with how I felt, or who I was at all. But this 'real self' was inarticulate, felt huge and clumsy, empty and sad. I cried a lot in those months, with friends and alone with my diary. I missed my sober Rick terribly and really wanted to know what was happening to him. I resented Marianne for her sanctions against contact, but stuck to it.

Gradually, however, in trying to refrain from being 'helpful', I began to realise how much of our relationship had been based on my 'rescuing' Rick. Without this function, I was plunged back into feeling needy myself, and became aware of how often I sought 'mothering' from other people. If I wasn't rescuing, I wanted to be rescued myself. When this wasn't forthcoming from my therapist one turning-point of a day, I suddenly came to and found that in all the tears and depression I wanted her to magically take away, there was a deep and volcanic rage. I knew I'd cry in therapy, but then I'd been crying for years in the face of even the mildest conflict, what I hadn't realised, was that I'd uncover feelings that were so frightening.

Once I had recognised the anger, I seemed to be aware of it all the time, like some terrible, unfocussed, vicious energy just below the skin. I began to be afraid I'd suddenly lose control and tear into anyone who happened to be near by. I felt I was going mad. I remember sitting in a cinema one night feeling as if at any moment I might start attacking the people around me. I had terrible dreams of murdering people, of dead bodies and bones. Staying focussed on myself seemed to realise my worst fears – that instead of just a nothingness inside, there was a cruel and vengeful violence. My therapist helped me realise that as so little anger had been allowed in my parental home, what I was now experiencing, as if for the first time, was rage in its most primitive infantile form, unmodified by the containment secure parenting can offer.

Then, little by little, the anger began to find a focus, and become less frightening. I was angry at Rick, who had left owing me a lot of money, which now, in my student and part-time working life, I badly needed. I felt furious – at last! about something! – that he had broken his promise to repay me, and that that was still having a substantial effect on my life; at my parents, for all the ways I felt they had blocked my attempts to become my own person, not with overt anger, but with a hostile, punishing silence and automatic nos. I dreamt of glaciers and icebergs and vast landscapes covered in thick snow. I started to sleep-walk – something I hadn't done for years – waking up at the window in a panic and feeling trapped and stifled. I was angry at myself for not having the guts to live the kind of life I somehow knew I could, if only I was brave enough to find out and go after what I really wanted, regardless of other people's approval. I was angry at, and envious of, women in general, whom I felt had the secret of being 'real women' smugly locked up inside themselves. And lastly, I was angry at society and at the fates at large, which had determined that life was so unfair, that so much potential was blighted.

Being aware of my anger at least enabled me to stop being so afraid of Rick, or feeling so responsible for him. I began to be able to see where my responsibility lay for what had happened; he was responsible for his drinking, and for his abusive behaviour towards me; but I was responsible for having allowed him to believe that that behaviour was acceptable to me. I had continually 'forgiven' him, understanding and making excuses for him, instead of refusing to collude with a blatantly worsening situation. My murderous thoughts had been a reflection of what I really felt, but had been unable to consciously register, or begin to express.

I do not blame myself for this; I did what I was able to at the time, given my past experience. But now I had to learn to stop doing it. I had to learn to say no. It wasn't easy. My feelings were so buried that I couldn't even register the possibility of *thinking* 'no'. My guts were somehow incorrectly tuned and I had to learn to trust that this would not always be the case.

A couple of years later I had an experience that showed me that trust was well founded. A man I had only met recently called me in a depressed state, wanting to see me and saying there was no one else he could talk to. When I put down the phone, having said he could come over, I had a strange feeling, one which, before, I might have registered as pleasure at being 'special' enough to be asked, together with a kind of excitement. But now I recognised it as fear. Something told me that I must not allow this man into my flat. So I met him on the doorstep, took him for a walk, and when he asked why I wouldn't let him in I told him that I thought he'd find it very difficult to leave. The verbal abuse that followed was sickeningly familiar. But when he had driven off in anger, telling me I had treated him like a dog, I realised I was feeling extremely happy. I had felt afraid, but I hadn't told myself I was being silly and should be more understanding – I had acted on the fear. The wisdom I had borrowed from Marianne and my therapist was really becoming my own.

Dealing with such situations satisfactorily is only half the battle – not getting into them in the first place takes longer. Continuing to focus on myself, taking time alone to do so, however selfish it has sometimes seemed, has been the only route to finding an inner security and what I now feel is my 'true' voice. There are many other things which have helped: getting to know some very different women through my course and at work, women who are fighting their own battles, neither looking for knights in shining armour to rescue them, nor little boys to take care of. They are proud of themselves, their bodies, their lives. They offer support and challenge, rather than 'rescue'. Over time, I have found my own strength. I try to use the envy I still feel sometimes as a pointer to aspects of myself I'd like to develop. Now I'm involved creatively on many fronts, at home and at the work I really enjoy. Once those good things seemed unreachable.

My body has changed, mostly through exercise, which has become both an essential and an enjoyable part of taking care of myself. I don't think I knew I had legs until I was 32 – both literally and metaphorically. My wardrobe is completely different – much more 'me' – a reflection of feeling much more 'in synch' with myself.

I have learnt to stay in the same place and same job, rather than moving on if things get too close or too 'samey'; to find something to value in all situations, rather than heading off for yet another idealised horizon. At the same time, I am learning when to leave, to claim my own space, to enjoy being alone. I don't feel that I am ready yet for a long-term committed relationship, but I feel that my choice of company of all kinds is healthier. Life generally feels richer and more real. In the one major relationship I had after Rick, I found I had to battle again with the murderous fantasies. Those fears, now fading, are an indication of my betrayal of myself, the killing of my truth. If I act on what I really feel, risk a conflict, say what I need to, I am true to myself.

I did meet Rick, by chance, sufficient time afterwards to hope that if there were a god or goddess he or she would look after him. I knew, at last, that I could not. Leaving that relationship was one of the hardest things I have ever done – but the consequences have had a profound effect on my life. From so nearly drowning in the distorted world of alcohol, I have learnt to stand more solidly on my own ground.

PICK OF THE JUMBLE

Linda Gould

Heaps of colourful jumble surround me in the spacious, tatty vicarage living room. Tomorrow is the annual Harvest Festival gala and I, vicar's wife and Jumble Sale Organiser *par excellence*, am sorting, categorizing and pricing.

I upend a huge black bag brought by Lil's grandchildren this morning. Rev. Rob, my old man, presided at her funeral yesterday. Funerals are what he's best at, especially the wakes where they serve whisky three fingers' deep in Tesco tumblers. In Lil's bag I expect to find the crimplene suits she wore to Family Service; nylon blouses and acrylic jumpers; an antique assortment of underwear, one-legged girdles and corsets and cast-iron bras; loads of lacy hankies and sachets of lavender soap; maybe some camiknickers and definitely Damart Thermolactyl underpants.

I'm in for a surprise. Out tumbles the most gypsy-spangled gaudy array of buttons and ribbons and elastic; diamante fabric strips, and page-three-model-type slinkies and kinkies – split-crotched bikinis and G-strings and basques with Page Three double D and double E cups, some cupless; sequinned dildoes and even a jockstrap-like contraption that plays 'Move Closer' when I touch it.

Good on you, Lil! You kept your secret well.

I imagine a parishioner barging in . . . 'Linda, you're a hero! What *would* we do without you?'

'Don't kid yourself, honey,' I reply, talking aloud to myself and Lil's ghost. 'I only do it for the pick of the jumble.' This time the unrivalled prize is a pearly pink mink-collared leather coat with those bracelet-length sleeves they used to wear with long kid gloves. I ponce around in it, thinking of wealthy Jewish ladies from Bethnal Green, wondering who wore it last, imagining what my friends in Lynx will say if I keep it.

Yep. Pick of the jumble. Stay with it, Linda.

Stay with Rob. You decided, with the therapist, that this was what you both wanted – to stay for the kids and the big tall skinny gothic brickheap you're committed to.

Stay with the status you're so reluctant to admit matters, the security you pretend to scorn. Forget your newfound love for women – not that it's wrong, but you've got priorities. Forget Rob's chronic affairs. He promised in therapy to give them up. You won't be the first or the last to manage – you're tough.

Stay. You can be sure you'll get no marks for honesty if you scarper. Stay.

I'm singing *Stay-ay-ay-ay Just a Litttttle bit Longer*. Giggles turn to laughter turn to tears. Usually I cry best in company. Now I'm alone, but I sob and sob. The vicarage – seventeen rooms not counting the butler's pantry – is so big that none of its numerous inhabitants hear.

I decide, then and there amidst the jumble, to stay with Rob; with his job and home and peccadilloes and his misuse of money, mostly mine. I decide to ignore the state of our relationship.

Even my dearest friend Sue is trying to save this marriage. 'You and Rob are superglue,' she says. 'Remember after death comes resurrection. Remember your optimism when you moved to the East End ten years back.' Another friend says, 'He only has flings to affirm his deepest love for you.' What tosh! And Rob? He says, 'You can have your relationship with

Daisy. Just be discreet, I can cope, we'll get there. Everything I do is for you.'

This he tells me on the day after confessing his latest dalliance – with a parish worker who (surprise, surprise!) I thought to be one of my best friends. I discover later that our twelve-year-old son knew of this affair. I am Humpty Dumpty after the fall. There I am, splat!

I try discretion. I finish my book by deadline. The editor likes it. I get pregnant. At thirteen weeks I lose the baby. I go to bed and don't get out. Friends, family arrive. 'Linda, snap out of it,' they say. 'You can get pregnant again. Don't throw the baby out with the bath water.' A tiny voice inside me squeaks 'It's not the baby. I've thrown out the baby and I'm drowning in the bathwater.' The doctor's note described my condition as 'general malaise': *'Allo allo! I'm your new staff officer General Malaise, meet my colleagues Major Depression, Serjeant Slightly Down, and Private Suffering. And not to forget Colonel Angst!'*

After three months I rise like a battered phoenix from my bed to return to the land of the living. I know that staying will be the death of me.

Discretion is the first casualty of this realisation. Rob is the only man I've ever slept with. I was a stubborn resister to sixties' permissiveness, and he has been a tender lover, but I feel I've come home in Daisy's arms. She is my first woman lover. I move from my shared bed with Rob to the bed settee in the lounge. Daisy joins me, often. We make love like Come Dancing. I've never done it before, yet it is so familiar – fun and funny, delicious, beautiful, good. Humpty is whole again. All women become beautiful to me – child to granny I love you all. How can they call this deviant?

The marital bedroom is directly above the lesbian love nest. I think 'Now he knows how it feels.'

I tell him, 'Making love to a woman is totally different,

better.' Even at the time I am stunned by my capacity for cruelty. Rob puts up with it; he is not a violent man. His pain is palpable. I push my luck. I am not the hero of this episode.

Nor am I discreet about the lifeguard at the women's pond. It is a breathlessly hot day, the last week of May, temperature touching 80 degrees and feeling like 95. School is a hothouse, so daughter Rosy and I head for the pond. Rupert the wild cockerel greets us from his perch in the giant oak. I spot her from the top of the shady path. She's wearing a turquoise blue bikini top and white boxer shorts so loose on her spare tanned middle that the waistband slips below her belly button. A white baseball cap perches crooked atop a dark tan pixie face. She watches us approach, toying with the whistle round her neck. I am thunderstruck. My heart races. I blush like a young thing. I want to nibble her ear.

'Gidday!' She grins as if she knows us.

'You a swimmer, then?' she asks Rosy, who informs her proudly that she's been swimming in the pond like a fish since she was seven which was *millions* of years ago. This is an important fact to establish, the women's pond being no place for non-swimmers or beginners. Nor, judging by my rushing pulse, for indiscreet vicars' wives.

'Tell you what,' she says to Rosy, 'it's pretty quiet now. How about I tow you round the pond on the lifebuoy? There's the moor hen's nest, sweetest little chooks you've ever seen.'

Kate tugs Rosy and I swim alongside as we circumnavigate the pond. The green-brown silky water soothes like a lover. We exchange phone numbers. Before I go, Kate invites me for a pint. Later at the pub we talk nonstop about our partners – she of her beautiful poet lover, I of my crazy vicarage life and Rob and the kids. This is not what we want to talk about and we both know it.

Home to the vicarage kitchen I float. Rob is chopping onions for chili con carne. 'Guess what?' I announce. 'I've just fallen in love with a lifeguard!' 'Lucky chap,' says Rob. 'At the women's pond,' I say. 'Oh!' says Rob.

Things get seriouser and seriouser with Kate. All the clichés come true – the first kiss, firework emotion, 'I feel I've known you forever,' 'I don't know where I end and you begin,' 'I am healed in your loving,' 'You are my everything.'

Snorkeling at sunrise, the warm mist lifting, lifting, through our masks we make underwater body jokes, Kate's imitation of Jaws, mine of a pike in sunglasses. We shed our togs and tie them to the lifebuoy, naked and whole.

> *Water woman, anemone, wash over me*
> *With your sweet body, ravish me.*

I tell Daisy about Kate. She says she knew anyway. Rob seems resigned when I tell him I must move away. He does not ask me to stay. His pain turns to cold hostility. For the first time I see in his face the price paid for our move to the East End: the grinding erosion of the optimism that buoyed us up in the early years, replaced by a mean kind of fatigue more and more frequently broken by bouts of drunkenness, terrible tantrums.

I begin spending nights at Kate's flat, returning to the vicarage each morning to collect Rosy for school, getting very little sleep.

We arrange our last Christmas together in the vicarage, goose with plum stuffing, the works. Kate is there, plus old friends. It is the most heartaching and gruesome day of my life. Still we all pretend to be happy. In the afternoon Rob goes off to his latest girlfriend's. We don't handle things well.

New Year brings resolution, not peaceful. One morning when I return from Southwark to collect Rosy for school, Rob is slicing cheese with a huge knife. I ask if Rosy's ready yet and he snaps. He approaches me angrily, shaking the knife in my face. Rosy skips into the kitchen. Rob keeps shaking the knife, too close for comfort, and I ask him please to put the knife down because it frightens me. Rosy starts crying, 'Please don't. Mummy, Daddy – please stop.' Rob says he is fucking not threatening me with the fucking knife and shakes it closer in my face and I repeat please please put it down we need to talk. Rob says why don't you just fucking move the hell out of here go shack up with that slag of yours south of the river! I run from the kitchen in terror, Rosy swooped under my arm.

Clearly, now is well past time to make a move. Rob is at a conference on reconciliation. I send Rosy for a weekend with a pal. My friends organise me on very short notice: fold and pack, pack and fold, tote that barge, lift that bale. An amazing collection of women, diverse and kind. Mandy's a Private Investigator; Helen a biker who wants to open a flower shop for rejected lovers (called *Terror Flora – with fronds like ours who needs anemones?* –); Suzanne, a telephonist-weightlifter who looks like a movie star and can climb walls like Spiderwoman; Jeanie, poet and computer typesetter; Maria, courier and accountant; Bryony, Greenham cronie and genius. And, of course, my beloved lifeguard.

I move into a housing association flat near Kate. Maria and Kate brighten Rosy's room with a slap of bright paint. The house is squalid: the loo leaks murky smelly goo on the concrete bathroom floor; live wires protrude dangerously, like broken nerves, in most of the rooms; the other adult in the house is genially mad, doesn't feed her two toddlers very often or seem at all concerned about hygiene.

For six months I survive, just, working in London's richest neighbourhood teaching rich kids, counting the days till June when Kate and I plan a move to the Shires. I think of the thousands, without money or friends, in ruinous relationships without hope of escape. What would I have done without education, money, privilege? Gone back to bed and not got out again? Or let that knife find its way to my face?

We hire a hunky Ryder truck and westward ho we go, Kate

and Rosy and I, with all our worldly goods and the cats and our beloved dog.

That will be three years ago tomorrow. I can tell you, hand on heart, that I've never known such happiness. Okay, I found out who my friends were. Some, who I thought I could count on, have disappeared, just not responding to letters and phonecalls. Others, from whom I expected nothing, have loved me like a rock. New, rich friendships have formed.

My partnership with Kate, how to begin? Sex is wonderful; we are open and honest. We are absolutely clear that we want a monogamous relationship, an arrangement not particularly important or relevant to many of our friends but essential to us.

All is not roses. I almost lost the house, and there are huge accumulated debts to pay off. One result of Rob's despair – right back while I was living with him – was that he stopped opening letters and cancelled his portion of the mortgage without telling me. Then he failed to use money from an insurance claim to pay off creditors. We were taken to court and I didn't even know about the hearing. Friends came to the rescue again when bailiffs threatened to pounce, shifting my precious computer and the telly, giving me time to sort out payments to the court.

I signed on for Income Support. Became fearless. I lost a commission to write a textbook, and started on my first novel. I got myself a wonderful agent.

Rosy is intensely unhappy and jealous and confused about my loving a woman and takes it out mainly on Kate. She tells school friends that Kate is our *au pair*. We are still working on this one. Some day, my darling Rosy, I know you will understand. She sees her papa every weekend and on holidays. Our divorce will go through this summer, joint custody, no financial strings for Rob. He is a loving father and I would like to be friends again but he remains very angry.

But we are on our feet. Kate runs a thriving business on a shoestring, and I have returned to a London job for one year only. Then I'll be free to be a poor proud writer in the Shires.

I recall the words of a sweet poem:

It's the heart afraid of breaking
that never learns to dance.
It's the dream afraid of waking
that never takes the chance.
It's the one who won't be taken
who cannot seem to give
And the soul afraid of dying that never learns to live.

They run some smashing jumble sales round these parts. The thought of a bargain still draws me like a magnet, but now I'm content to be a punter. I don't miss the pick of the jumble at all.

EROSION

Katie Campbell

Watching a marriage
flailing,
fail

when the relationship
and the failure
is you

is having your image
erased
from a rock face:

slowly, softly
the rain
relentlessly

scraping
everything
away.

A NEW SENSE OF INDEPENDENCE

Belona Rix

There were no concrete reasons for the end of my ten-year marriage to Kasimir. He was and is a remarkable and unique individual who has displayed an awesome strength and courage in the two years since our separation began. It was difficult for the people around us to understand my reasons for leaving, since they were so abstract, connected to a spiritual, emotional and practical progress. The one person who did seem to understand was the man I was leaving.

The decision was brought to a head by the increasingly disastrous state of our mutual finances, and my endemic fatigue. We lived in comparative squalor, sharing a house in Brixton with a couple whose unstable rages regularly wrecked every window on the premises. I was working on a small magazine and as a news monitor, two jobs which were equally exhausting, and I was trying to entice some creative activity out of my husband who had sunk into a state of total inactivity. It was this inability for us to work together any more, me surging forward with little thought but enormous amounts of nervous energy and him more ponderous and, at times, deeply pessimistic, that sounded the death knell on what had been, at times, an incredible shared history.

I started to dread going home. I began to create a vision of an independent life, imagining a state I had not experienced since I had settled down with Kasimir at the age of eighteen. Kasimir had grown frightened of the outside world, unable to try to find work to help reduce the financial pressure I was under; unable to help to find us somewhere else to live; unable to find the courage, in effect, to take some decisive step to improve the quality of our lives. I could see no way out. I felt I had tried everything. If I went on like this, I would be dead of frustration and exhaustion in five years and would never be able to fulfil my ambitions. I wanted to break while there was still love between us, with the hope that we would, one day in the future, be able to be friends.

In August, Kasimir went to stay in North Wales, on holiday from what I resentfully perceived was his full-time leisure. I was working in the suffocating heat, writing wheedling letters to the bank and living out of bags in the houses of different friends, since the thought of returning to our home, swamped with heroin and violence, was unbearable.

I will never forget his leaving. I will never forget the pain, the responsibility I felt for inflicting such cruelty on another, as well as on myself. There was some music playing on the radio in the kitchen and we danced together in tears. He begged me not to send him away. It was the hardest thing I have ever done, to walk away into the garden, to turn my back and stick to my resolution as he left the house. I sat in a state of shock in the heat, repeating to myself, 'I've done it, I don't believe it, I've done it,' while a sense of total isolation swept over me. I must have sat for an hour in rigid paralysis, watching the chickens at the end of the garden viciously picking at each other, watching the small movements of insect life in the grass and in the air, feeling a strange buzzing sensation surround my body. I imagined working out of a small flat near Lamb's Conduit Street or Notting Hill, or working on a cruise ship as a croupier in exotic locations, and found a momentary sense of relief.

Then I went to work. To keep my resolve high, I listened

to music on my Walkman. I managed not to cry, but at work, as the sweep of computers and TV and video screens filled my vision, I broke down under the glare of all things familiar. A friend brought me a bottle of whisky and it was this and the demands of work that got me through the night. The long and feverish battle against emotional collapse had begun.

I used several devices, in those early days, to help me survive: I would tell myself, as I was fighting back tears on the haul to work, that I was my mother's daughter, no weakening; and I clung to an abstract sense of fate. I spilled out all the confusion and misery to this faceless but benignly spiritual presence.

I look back on those first three months with a quiet amazement at the fact that I did survive. I was sleeping on various friends' floors while trying to find some affordable home. I had little privacy and since it had been instilled in me since youth that there was no room for fuss or self-pity, I did my grieving in short, secret moments. There must be no crying, if it could be helped, before others.

I lost many friends. One man I had known for eight years asked me if I would like to go to bed with him for half an hour, two days after Kasimir had left. Another put me under such intense sexual pressure that I had to start avoiding him, until our friendship ended in anger. I knew in my heart that I needed to be alone to discover myself but, instead, answering a strange call of adventurism, I entered into a disastrous short-term affair with a former Chinese film star, whose appetite for me stopped short after sex and who donated absolutely zero in terms of human support. I felt like a flesh factory.

I emerged from my long marriage feeling dreadfully naïve. I felt desperately uncertain about what I had done; a terrible temptation to turn back. I suffered from the sudden loss of sharing things. Although I was twenty-eight years old, I was innocent. I was open to abuse and received it.

Imagining that I was really living, I allowed myself to be diverted from my intention of going home to see my mother for some old-fashioned comfort, to the dubious benefits of a hotel bedroom farce in Cornwall. Suddenly I was having to face the unfamiliar feeling of being single with sexual desires, an awful, surging restlessness which was probably more a need for some affectionate human contact than a demand for physical release.

But at last I found a home and began to come to terms with being on my own. I had to rework all the hidden grief, all the misery I had kept dormant while I was staying with different friends. In my new stable environment, I was able to examine my entire past. I was very poor since most of my wages were being used to pay off the bank, but I was determined not to give in, no matter what problems arose. I would repeat to myself, and still do, 'I will not be defeated, I will not be defeated. I am my mother's daughter, for God's sake! I have the mark of Napoleon.' Bizarre, perhaps, but it worked.

Gradually, I started to enjoy being alone, feeling, as each month passed, that I was getting a little stronger. I got so bored with being miserable that it became easier to start being happy. I was working through the nights as a news editor, which was physically and mentally demanding but rewarding, and was trying to write in the days. I filled up my life with work and discovery, and finally decided to discard any limitations on the possibilities that the future might present. I decided on one major ambition: the pursuit of a genuine happiness and to be a tough old bird by the time I was forty.

I also decided to live and work abroad. I wanted to have the courage to give up everything – my home, my friends, my possessions – to stand in a new landscape with nothing but my sense of independence. It was the search for this liberty, to be strong, to be essentially honest, that led to the end of my marriage. It has now led me from Berlin to Italy, to enthusiasm, to excitement, to days long on hope.

OWNING YOUR LIFE

Cathy Symmonds

There is a feeling – not so much of being in control – but of owning your own life again.

I had never, in all my married life, felt as though I owned anything. Even the house was his. I was worn out with the effort of compromising (or more accurately, arguing furiously), then being beaten into silence. The plants, the dog, the wallpaper, the microwave, the freezer, the holiday to be planned, 'the in-laws' to be visited, the children to be born – were all his.

Eventually you forget who you are, you get lost and you tear yourself in two, trying to live out someone else's life.

But being alone is terrifying. Just you – who the hell are you? A bruised stranger needing help.

> Awed by the selfness of it –
> Your books, your things,
> that rug, you chose it,
> mistakes – your mistakes,
> all yours,
> your bills,
> your discovery,
> yourself.

Three days after leaving my husband, a girl was shot outside my front door, her stomach, along with her morals, splayed out for all to see, on the pavement. Late at night, as I was dragged into consciousness by two burly policemen, I realised what I had done. I had exchanged my nice cosy, comfortable existence, where the only sound on the early morning air was the buzz of lawnmowers busily tidying up neighbours' lives, for one where anything could happen. This was Sheffield, with its college and university and cathedral, and someone had been shot on my doorstep for refusing to buy drugs. And I had left my husband, whom I loved, to come here.

> 3 a.m.
> The face in the mirror
> stares out at me
> looking as I do
> for your yellow toothbrush.

You bargain with yourself.

'He's wrong, he's wrong, we can make it work. With some effort and changes we can work it out.'

'What about sex?'

'Sex doesn't matter, friendship is more important.'

But what about sex? It'll happen again. Remember the times, the awful times, the awful fear that he might find you attractive, might demand sex. You know you don't want him. You know your body is telling the truth. You know everything in you is screaming 'No'. Only your lips are framing the word 'Yes'.

Why did you lie to him, to yourself, to your body, say: 'Here I am, have me, buy me, take me'? You wanted to believe that yours was a normal relationship, that you did the normal things that married people do, that you made love and that everything was all right. But when you found something that really touched you, that really made you live and think and breathe again, then you couldn't lie. Then you had to go.

I auditioned for a play and my life changed. I woke up to creativity, politics, culture, sex – my life utterly, irrevocably and completely changed.

There was nothing I could do to stop it – the whole lie I had been living came bursting out.

> You didn't ask me what I thought and so
> I didn't tell you.
> it not being fair, to force one's
> thoughts on one unwilling, and yet
> though foetal, yet in thought
> it had a future which could force
> its way through
> lips unwilling
> and splutter out against your face.

I told you I didn't love you, and then I left you.

His name was David, and he changed my life.

> my husband doesn't understand me
> but I don't love my husband . . .
> It's cosy in the cupboards,
> last year's boots,
> a scarf he bought me
> as a love-you present,
> old handkerchiefs, and scraps of lace,
> we'd meant to make a collage,
> or embroider a mirror's edge,
> or something.

But we didn't. I went looking for a flat, and found one in the red light district. I was to have a room with two windows, one facing East and one West. It felt right, I was getting morning and afternoon sun. I was getting something I had never had.

Loneliness was something new. I spent evenings, long stretched-out spaces of time, willing myself back into marriage, but always knowing at the back of my head it would never be.

> So here we are
> Head hunting.
> Viz me with spear and appropriate
> war paint
> you, with flank, presented,
> but doe-eyed, twitching
> occasionally presenting rump.

To try and create more space between us, I tried to force myself into shoes too narrow, dresses too tight. I made friends with unsuitable people and went out to places I didn't like. It felt wrong and it kept forcing me back to you.

> as if orange juice, comprehensive
> schools and Habitat rugs
> made any difference.

For a while I was lost, thrashing around, trying to grow up, grafting on to a life, once mature, something new and different. At twenty-five I began to change, and experienced all the losses associated with being an adult with emotional lags. Lags which came from growing next to a bigger, better plant, that took your water, took your space and took your light.

Going through my post-adolescent adolescence
– growth not expected, the baby bulge,
but growth, nevertheless.
Rocketed from the careful tracks of
fairground
intricacies, to the black hole of swamp
and secret,
of course, there was the splash of cold,
as we dashed towards the end
of hopes, crashed
with a paid-up fare and,
end of ride parade.

You were a catalyst, a focus for my future, a lamppost on
my street. But you had your own mark to make. You wanted
to experience me, to grow up on me, but, ultimately, I was
a landmark and your journey was with someone else, to
somewhere else.

I brought you some tulips
– there were five, I think,
no more in a bunch today.
You looked at me as if to say,
'Why came in with the sunlight
and last year's leaves?'
But politeness prevailing
we talk a while.
She said
You look at her
with your cardigan falling
away from your shoulder
and that your smile is sudden
warming your face.

I experienced the sharpness of jealousy, the desperateness of wanting someone who wanted someone else. When I saw you, my insides exploded. I left my stomach on the pavement and you smeared the blood as you walked away.

I caught a corner of your room.
Some step-ladders said
You'd moved
or perhaps decorated.
On the bus, you could only see a bit,
until it went past.
At the weekend I walked past,
the yucca was back
the curtains half-drawn
like before
you asleep, I suppose on the bed
by the window.
I thought of the fresh morning coffee
you carefully brewed
in our two chipped mugs.
When we met, you said
you were at the top of the step-ladders;
but you'd already turned out the light.

You left me and in that loss, I finally grew up.

FROM HERE TO THERE

Janet Craze = Teacher

This afternoon I put up a new curtain rail with my own electric drill in my own house, went out for a brisk walk, dropped in on a good friend (male) for a cup of tea and walked home feeling cheerfully at ease with myself, my children and my little part of the world. Small achievements perhaps, but significant to me.

Five years ago I was in hell. On New Year's Day 1986 my husband finally admitted that there was another woman, somebody he had met through work. The next three months, while he decided whether to stay or go, were fiercely destructive. He blamed me for driving him to extra-marital affairs, citing my frigidity, my lack of humour, my grim and joyless approach to life. I felt numb and became totally passive. I felt out of control, worthless, rejected. I was physically and emotionally terrified of my husband: I started swigging from the brandy bottle at five each evening and shook when I heard his key in the door. Somehow I maintained some semblance of normality for the children and so that I could go on with my part-time teaching job.

When, at Easter, my husband finally left, my emotions were mixed. Part of me felt relief that I would not have to face those bitter, undermining verbal attacks; the rest felt pure physical pain – a precise pain in the chest which made me breathless.

49

At night I would fall heavily asleep in exhaustion, only to jerk wide awake an hour later with my heart pounding and my mouth dry. Terrified of destitution, I would run round the house hiding money – the building society passbook in my Latin dictionary, a £5 note under the bedside rug. When I slept again I dreamed about him – that he was back, that he was loving and affectionate, as before. When I was awake I talked to him endlessly; unspoken conversations ran in my head. Obsessed with the past, I went over and over old diaries and photographs, reassessing memories, trying to make sense of what didn't make sense. I flirted with suicide, reading coroner's reports, fitting the vacuum cleaner hose to the car exhaust. I drove dangerously, willing something to happen to me. On such occasions I felt that I could not continue through the next half-hour, let alone through the rest of my life. I could see no way through.

It is odd, five years on, to look back at that demoralised and demented woman. I have a full-time job and my own house and car; I have plenty of friends and, until recently, a lover. I have tried sailing, rock 'n' roll dancing and watercolour painting. I feel lively and independent and I am happier with myself than I have ever been before. How did I get here from there? A major turning point was the moment I found I could laugh about it. I remember gloomily telling a friend that my husband was in love with a half-Japanese co-counselling sex therapist. Then the funny side struck us both and we giggled immoderately. By the time my husband's new house needed underpinning, I was able to make cheerfully acid comments about how the earth had moved once too often for him.

My friends were a huge support. My oldest friends, who had known me before my marriage, reminded me that I had been my own person before and would be again. An old schoolfriend phoned me faithfully every week for months and let me pour out my heart to her. Another came to stay for a week when my husband first left and helped with the children. I was invited out to drinks, meals and theatres – it all helped. I made many new friends: there is something about going through a major experience which breaks down barriers. I had wonderful letters from all sorts of people. I copied out extracts on cards and re-read them at low points to remind myself how many people thought well of me.

Building up self-esteem was difficult. It is shattering when the person who knows you best on earth, your companion over twenty years, the father of your children, your best friend, turns on you and tears you apart. Being lied to destroys your self-respect. Friends who tell you that you are okay, who see you in a different light, are crucial. So were my children. At first I tried not to cry in front of them but they always knew when I was upset. Almost before I was aware of my own distress, I would find my son in my lap or my daughter's hand in mine. 'How did you know?' I asked later. It was a while before they told me that the tip of my nose glowed red when I felt emotional.

But the children were a source of stress as well as of comfort. Both of them were very attached to their father and felt that he had rejected them as well as me. My nine-year-old daughter cried herself to sleep every night for a year; my son, three years younger, had nightmares and reverted to bed-wetting. (I felt bitter, changing sheets at three in the morning, while my husband slept with his new partner. I wish now I had had the spirit to send the drenched sheets to them.) My abiding sadness about this time is that when the children most needed a rock to lean on, I was least able to be it.

But in the last five years our relationship has developed in different directions. I can't play the protective Earth Mother that I wanted to be, but I can be myself. I've learned to say that I do my best and my best is sometimes lousy. They are tolerant of my shortcomings; they know that I get ratty, burn the broccoli with astonishing regularity and shriek when they spill coffee on the carpet. For their part, my son (now twelve) consults me about his burgeoning love life and my daughter engages in midnight discussions about life and the universe. I feel trapped by them at times, but I feel sorry for my ex-husband, who misses out on so much.

I have also grown closer to my parents since he left. They have given me practical and emotional help, visiting to look after the children, and giving me money too. In the first few months my father phoned me every night at bedtime, just to say goodnight. My mother, a kindly Christian lady who never speaks ill of anybody, helped me by her rage against my husband. The day she said, shaking with emotion, '*Damn* him!' was the day I first began to accept that I was not totally to blame for everything that had gone wrong. I had a period when I felt intensely angry with my parents – and with my mother in particular – for the unrealistic ideas about life and marriage which they had instilled in me. But that passed. At the crunch, they were there and there for *me*.

I was extremely fortunate in getting help from a strong, warm and perceptive Relate counsellor. My underlying problems were guilt and low self-esteem. Over the months, we were able to trace these emotions back to childhood and lay the ghosts to rest – more or less. The experience was painful beyond anything but I knew that it was therapeutic. My counsellor used to say that we don't get what we want in life but we do get what we need. Eventually I was able to accept that the marriage had become destructive to me as well as to my husband and that we both needed it to end.

I still wish that it hadn't had to happen this way. I still feel sadness and loss. I still feel bitter at times. It's hard to accept that such feelings won't disappear magically. There are times when I am overtired or stressed and feel close to collapse again, but I know that I have come through. And when I look back to myself before the marriage breakdown, and consider what I have learned and gained since, I know too, that I would never go back.

LOVE LETTER TO MY SON

Clare Venables

You have gloriously buggered up my life.

Your perfect head
explodes firecrackers
in my quiet life.

The curve of your leg from hip to thigh
trembles my knees.

Your bony ankles –
not a feature I give much thought to
in others –
are frail supports for my passion.

I can't keep the ten commandments
any longer. Because of you
pain blood and torture
stalk my dreams and burst into
violent life. I'd murder for you.

It's not a pleasant thought
in a civilised person.

LETTING HER GO

Za   = Teacher

I am all pain, all panic. She is killing me. I am frightened. I walk by the sea and the pebbles shine and merge. I can't stop crying. There are people and dogs and children and seagulls around me but they seem very far away. I feel so alone. My throat is tight with pain. The pain is bursting in me. I sit in the car and watch the picture-book people and dogs in the sun, glistening and merging. I just don't believe what's happening.

I've been crying all night and all day since her phonecall. Weeks ago I left her. But I could not bear to be away from her. I returned. She will not have me back. It's over. After eight years together. The most significant relationship of my life and I've chucked it all away.

Now I'm on the run. I haven't lived on my own for a long time. This is the one bright aspect. I delight in the peace and freedom it brings. In a rented cottage I pace up and down, talking out loud, going over and over our life together and how we might have got to this point. On teaching days, I get some respite. After work, the frantic pacing begins, again.

In another rented place I write, filling pages with all that I want to say to her, but never sending it. No one in the world knows I am in this numbed state of grief. Perhaps it is not really happening. I keep thinking I'll wake up and everything will be right again.

I'm desperate for a place of my own, a place to hide up in for ever like a wounded animal.

There is nowhere I feel at home. These temporary spaces are expensive but they give me somewhere to do my planning – a place I can leave behind with all its associations of this unreal time.

I plan for a nest in which to do my crying. I have so much crying to do. Something more horrible is about to happen to me, I'm sure of it. I can't stop it, but I'm trying to delay it until I can find a safe spot and no witnesses.

I have to hide the pain politely inside me. It becomes a burning secret. To tell could cost me my job and destroy her professional career.

Anyway, I am suddenly friendless. How can I be? I've always been someone who loves people and many have been drawn to me. Why am I looking at the rows of names in my address book and asking which of them are my friends? Whom can I trust? I want to tell them all that I've just split with her, that we've been lovers for years, that my heart is breaking.

I dare not say anything to family, friends or colleagues. I can't even share it with my own mother. If my lover had died it would have been the same. All my life, I've had lesbian relationships – before and during my long marriage and since my divorce. But I've led a double life and it has been a great strain.

Now I keep the covers on. Used to it. Done it since I was nine when my father deserted us. We were told to keep that secret too. My mother was ashamed of it.

So I pose now, all energy, shiny, brittle, determined. I take a really tough teaching job and I focus on the house I'm buying. I'm a smartly dressed zombie, sleek, masked, grinning, full of restrained pain. This is how I deal with it. The pattern was set long ago but it's going to take months before I really understand all this.

My creative work is unstoppable. I paint tree after tree with thick black acrylic branches. My nightmares are terrible. At work no one remarks on my swollen eyes.

At last I move into my own house.

I apply for Headships. This, I tell myself, is sensible. It certainly looks good, especially when I'm shortlisted for six. Status, high salary, more demanding responsibility for others – so right for an independent, strong woman. And that's what I am, surely?

I think a lot about when my father left. I was small and trusting. I loved him so much. My mother ran into the garden where I was playing. She was screaming hysterically and waving a letter in her hand. 'He's left me! He's left me!' she screamed. A neighbour came to comfort her.

I sat on the grass and watched my mother sobbing. I felt abandoned by him. Desolate. Grief-stricken. I was told to 'leave Mummy alone, don't keep clinging to Mummy, don't cry, be Mummy's good girl and make Mummy happy.' So I shut up and grieved inside for them both for years.

A young woman picks me up in the bar of the theatre. She is good-looking. Shall I take her home and let her fuck me in my new white room? New house, new job, new sex. Who cares? And I'm not looking for any love affair, not real love. Who wants this hell again? Not me, ever. No, I'm getting over this bloody misery. Doing fine.

I go for the Headship interviews, the first of several. Get on to a Diploma in Management course.

Then, suddenly, I hit death. I am broken, diminished to a speck, cut off from the world. Sobbing uncontrollably while I'm standing in Sainsbury's. It's Christmas. I lie to everyone, pretending I'm fine. I take the phone off the hook, and I cannot eat, cannot stop thinking of her. For weeks she has ignored me. Now she rings me, fights with me, will not let me go, but will not have me back. She is my tormentor. I hate her. Alone in my white house I scream at her, 'You fucking shitting bitch! You bloody fucking shit bag!'

I pray on my knees, Please God, Goddess, Creator of the Universe, I love her. Please make her forgive me, make her want to be with me as we were before. She is my beloved. I will never love anyone in the way that I loved her.

I want magic. I want spells. I am all wanting, all pain, a helpless child again. How can she abandon me like this?

I write letters, cancelling all remaining Headship interviews, drive to the postbox, sending cards to one and all describing how good life is. I don't want them intruding on this. I lock the door and start on the first bottle of whisky. I begin a journal, an hourly account of all that I feel. It is a terrible document, ranging over the whole of my life so far. I wonder whether I want to go on living.

A rash appears all over me. My joints hurt. I am vomiting. I cannot breathe. How tired I am.

For two weeks, I stay in my pyjamas. When I am not drunk, I paint and write and read Dorothy Rowe's compassionate and helpful books.

There are bills to be paid. I must eat. The telephone must ring. Soon I've got to face the world again. I miss my children. I want to hug them. They seem very far away.

Daffodils bloom in a bowl. Spring sunshine comes. I've always loved life, gone at it eagerly up to now, blighting and spoiling it with deception and compromise, but still experiencing so much joy.

When someone loved and trusted abandons you, it's like they've handed you your own death.

Suddenly, I feel a change in me, and a realisation that she too must have been suffering since I left her in the first place.

The childish prayers become meditation; the raging becomes exercise and yoga. These old familiars I now approach like a humbled beginner. The disciplined work begins with great stillness and great activity. It will take months, perhaps years.

Each day I rise early and write freely, a re-established routine which has taken on a new importance. I'm like a sort of crippled but enthusiastic phoenix rising. Exercise, meditation, baths of hot deep water with oils, and then work. At weekends I do strong physical labour, making my garden from scratch. I bake bread, bashing the dough violently, then gradually with more control. I allow no television, no radio, no newspapers or music. At night I read from sacred texts. I paint trees, black, then blue, then yellow and green with bright leaves. Please, Creator of this mysterious world, heal this friendship and support all those who grieve. That is all. I let her go. I pray that she is happy.

My children ring me, as concerned as always,

'Are you sure you're all right?'

'Yes,' I say truthfully, 'Don't worry. I'm coping well.'

Perhaps they know me better than I think. Perhaps. When I am more healed, I will try to talk to them.

I am less pale and skinny. The hours spent cooking tasty vegetarian food, served on my best china, caring for my surroundings, tending my garden, confiding all to my friendly cat, enjoying the colours and scents at the garden centre, relaxing with candles and incense, are making me well.

I'm singing happily in the car at the top of my voice. I walk by the sea in my wellies, wading along, thinking how strong I feel, how good it is to be alive. I marvel at the beauty of clouds and sea and seaweed.

Why such unhappiness over separation from one particular person? I begin to look at this question calmly, with real interest.

We were so much to each other: mother, father, sister, brother, child and lover. It was wonderful and terrible to be so much. You lose your unique self in all that, or you can do, if you never make space to be alone, to depend utterly on yourself.

We had so much fun, went through so much together, shared so much love. I will always appreciate how fortunate I was to be her partner. And now I am grown strong and independent again, and perhaps in a strange way she has made that possible too.

One night, I tear up thirty years of personal journals and burn them. A life lived. A life over. A decision. I will come out and present to the world my whole self.

The part-time job has been a good idea, though financially scary. There is only me to keep and I have other skills I can use to earn money. I take jobs cleaning, ironing, washing up, and I sell some writing and do other things.

Now I give priority to the real job instead of the proper job. I do my creative work without distortion and wish I'd had the courage to do so years ago. I'll encourage others to be braver from the beginning.

My garden plot does well. I pick flowers and turn up new potatoes and cut lettuce and cabbage and offer them as gifts. In school I laugh with pupils and colleagues and listen carefully to their problems. I walk slowly and calmly. Sometimes I swim long distances. I am patient with lonely people who want to talk. I visit family and friends.

My senses are reawakening. The smell of fruit and perfume and polish is lovely. The birds are singing. I notice them. I take off my clothes and feel the sun on my skin. Music is great to listen to again and doesn't make me sad – well, only sometimes.

I put out photos of loved ones, but not pictures of her, not yet. It's good to be with groups of women again, to laugh and discuss and join in activities. How easy it is to arrange to do this without guilt! So much that I wanted to do alone looked like disloyalty to my lover.

In longer and deeper periods of meditation, I confront my self and my past self and I unearth a new self that had been there all the time.

My self and I, we begin to have fun. We are into erotic affairs. These occasional flings are essential healing steps on my personal journey, and I will always remember these sexual partners. It was good to hear them say that I had helped them too.

And now?

I stand exhilarated and increasingly exposed. There are occasional moments of terror, for the memory of the worst days of this journey will remain forever. But I coped alone and surely I can do so in the future?

My time is used now with much reverence. Why am I doing this? I used to ask, but then I didn't listen to the answer. Now I ask the question daily and I listen and consider the answers before I act.

Time spent earning money is useful if the money is spent on things that are truly valuable to me. Time for people is mostly reserved for those who accept me and respect the real me. Self-disclosure is risky but it enables others to reveal more of themselves. I treasure my many friends.

The world is full of lovely things which satisfy my sensuality and stir my imagination, and people are always interesting.

Now I try to go for clarity in relationships. Let's talk. Tell me what you want. Lovers see what they'll get from me and they get what they see. Life is too short and too precious for complicated and confused relating. I've pared away so much. I need so little. I believe in happiness.

Older, wiser women teach me so much, and I try to give support to those who seek it – many do. I'm moved when I can enable younger lesbians to be braver than I was, and I feel compassion when I see that some are not as brave as I was.

My private space and times for meditation are sacred.

In stillness and focussing, I maintain the inner strength I have and the calm acceptance that in the end we are all alone.

So far, so good. The experience of separation has been agonising and extremely enriching. So all is hunky-dory? Surely yes. And not much is going to freak me? Right. And I like my own company and I'm this big strong independent woman? Right. And I know now how to keep it that way? Absolutely right. But, and I hardly can bring myself to say it, as it makes me feel sort of vulnerable – I've fallen in love! My new self boldly awaits the next stage of my journey.

LONELINESS

Sun Sun Lwin

I learned all about loneliness when I was a child sent away to boarding school. And I have never been free of the emotion.

My parents left for the Far East, having deposited me in a pleasant red-brick building wreathed in ivy and set amidst lawns and rhododendron bushes. The school was near the sea and every morning, with the mist, rolled in a heady smell of salt.

Assuaging loneliness and the sense of isolation has been a lifelong task. Actually, I think it started earlier than my experiences at St Vincent's, but memories fail me. Other people let me steal glimpses of my past. My mother saying, *You ʋ re so jealous when your sister was born. You would shout 'Go and feed that baby,' then run away and hide in your room for hours*. Her long-past exasperation, which leaked out on the telling of that story, made me wince still. Photographs show my father grinning, holding me, swinging me in the air and sliding me down the gradient of his legs, my father who was my first playground. Did the playing stop when Dil was born? Or did he start to stay away more then, on business trips, days spent at the office?

I enjoyed the intimacy yet curious lack of closeness in my marriage. Why else did I choose a man who could not reveal his emotions if not for the sense of familiarity it brought; the

62

belonging and warmth confined to bed, offshot by a distance both of us fought to maintain? He did not understand me as a whole person any more than I could view him holistically. I was segmented into a series of bits to be railed against and despised, or those which pleased him and could be boasted about to impress friends. I always felt I was living in his dream. I did not have the courage to live in my own.

After years I broke free. My father's death sealed the fate of the marriage. For once, the fact that I could not rely upon my husband mattered. I tried other relationships, lurching from one young lover to another. I found them safe. They were always impossible to be truly intimate with, not one of them could feed my hunger with their limited diet of life and love.

Then I met a Grand Passion. Young, like the others, and just as insufficient, but by now something in me was changing. I turned to him for support, but he ran from responsibility. I went through the traumas of moving house, being on the dole, losing my car, and finally cervical cancer. At each juncture I can safely say he was not there for me. Yet in a strange way I do believe that if he had been I would not have learned to be so strong and to find myself. He once told me that when he was a child of four he had watched his mother, bent over with exhaustion in the bathroom where she had been clearing up after him and his three other brothers and sisters, and recalled thinking, *She is going to die and I can't help her*. His father was on a four-year course in America and his mother had raised them single-handedly. He had been the most trouble of all the children – the third brother, always sickly with asthma. My lover watched me too, bent over with exhaustion, and remained as paralysed as he had been then, still embedded in a frieze of impotence.

I do believe that we choose people who can help us to make or break ourselves. I chose my husband and my lover to register my steel, to power my own destiny. And they chose me to help them break away from the limitations of their past. Who is to know when and where they or I will succeed.

What have I learned? I am not yet ready to fully trust another human being but I have begun to trust myself since my years of living on my wits to bring up my children and myself.

What has brought me lasting pleasure? My life forged from my own metal and skill; my children, their humour, resourcefulness, and sense of honour; my body, which responds with such transports to physical and emotional loving.

What shall I do? Continue to gain in understanding and experience so that one day, if I never meet a partner who can satisfy my needs, I shall be able to fuel my own world. I no longer have to isolate my self from people or make them afraid with the power of my fear.

I returned to St Vincent's, my old school, the other day. I walked past the buildings sheathed in trees, and along the seawall. It's no longer a school but a nursing home, where bewildered elderly people perambulate on lawns once strewn with children. I expected some Daphne du Maurier revelation, a sort of 'Mandalay Revisted'. But the smell of the salt air dredged up no long-buried sorrows, no regrets. The life which I had made since those days held far too much promise.

Roz Cowman

What else could she do, when that old fool,
pickled in prudence, holier than she,
God's loudspeaker, forced her to climb
up out of the plain, start again with him,
housewife to a tribe, getting back
to Nature as he called it, milking
his camels, hoarding their dung
for fuel, hearing him talk to his dreadful god
while the stars hummed like bees
in the white nights of the desert.

She was used to her oily kitchen
on the brawling street, the panniered donkeys,
dust-devils at corners, hawkers of fried cakes,
women with cures and curses,
littered courtyards, glossy young merchants
and soldiers in the market for discreet
invitations, suppers at twilight
on long terraces, with her
bawdy, middle-aged companions.

Of course she paused, there,
at the head of the pass, at sunset,

looked back, thinking
it over, then retraced her steps.
He, to save face, shouted some imprecation
about fiery rain, pillars of salt . . .
But she walked back, uncaring,
down to the great plain
and smoke of little cities on the evening air.

REGAINING CONTROL
AND SELF-RESPECT

Elaine Benson

I was seventeen years old when I got married – already the mother of a two-month-old baby, before that was fashionable. The pattern for my marriage was set on my wedding day. I should have been wary, but I was young and thought I was in love. If the truth be known, I had clung to the first person who had shown me any affection.

On my wedding night he dragged me home at 10 p.m. because he was drunk and tired. Meek me followed, like a lamb to the slaughter. The pattern established itself: him: out in the pub every night; me: stuck in the house with a baby and in debt because he stole the rent to go out drinking. He would come home and collapse in a drunken stupor on the living-room floor, or piss up the wall in the bedroom, when he made it that far.

Shortly after our first anniversary I left him and returned to my mother's. But I was too frightened, too insecure to stay. I went back to him.

On our third anniversary, in June 1979, my divorce petition went in. I was twenty years old and had two children: my daughter aged three and my son aged four months.

Then the real nightmare began. My husband refused to leave the house. I was forced to live with him while the divorce went through and for three months after. I was refused a 'quickie' divorce and had to have a formal court hearing. It took four months. During this time my husband continued to drink and was now even more abusive. Each night, before he went out, as he inevitably did, he threatened to beat me up on his return. When I knew the time for last orders had come I began to panic, knowing he would soon be home.

This went on for months; night after night. I was a complete wreck. He abused me, mainly emotionally, but also sexually and physically. He threatened to take the children away from me and unrelentingly attacked my self-confidence. *I* lost weight and all-but disappeared. But one night freed me. He arrived home very drunk and, after a brief argument, beat me up and tried to strangle me. A lucky knee into his crutch got him off me. The next day, bruised and sore, I went to see my solicitor. Due to the violence I got emergency legal aid and an emergency hearing for an injunction. He was ordered to leave the house within three weeks. The day he actually left was one of the happiest of my life. That first night, just me and the kids. No drunk coming home. No abuse. Just peace and quiet and calm. WOW!!

Perhaps the most difficult area for me to address is how I feel about myself now. I am only just becoming aware of myself as a person. That may sound strange, but until recently I wasn't even aware that I didn't think of myself as a whole complete person. I simply didn't think of myself at all. It is only through therapy that I am realising that I have repressed so much of myself. I did it because it was the only way that I could survive some of the horrors in my life. Only now am I realising how incredibly strong I am. I've always thought of myself as a weak, inadequate person. I felt that must be true since I had allowed myself to be abused in the ways I had. The abuse from my husband had compounded the continuous psychological and sexual abuse inflicted on me by the gang of boys I had hung around with as a teenager. To have survived all that intact and (relatively) sane is, indeed, amazing, I'm proud of myself for that.

Life as a single parent is often made difficult by the attitudes of others. I was very naïve. In the beginning I didn't realise that to some people single parents are anathema. I was confused when so-called friends from my married days ignored me. I became angry when men presumed that I was an easy lay because I had been married and was, therefore, used to having sex ('Once you've been used to it, you can't do without it').

It has taken me many years to begin to regain some control and self-respect. It began in 1984, five years after my divorce, when I finally plucked up the courage to go back to night school. I enrolled to do some 'O' levels. I was terrified. I was convinced that I didn't have the intelligence to pass the exams, and trying to do my first essay was a nightmare. But I was determined not to fail. I didn't want to feel like a failure any more. I passed all three 'O' levels with flying colours. After that success I was encouraged by the tutors to go for an 'A' level. Yet again I was convinced that I would never be capable of that standard of work – but what the hell! I had nothing to lose. To my astonishment, I passed that too. I began to wonder just what I was capable of. I'd never pushed myself like this; I'd always been too frightened, too insecure, convinced I was a total failure, a nothing. And yet, here I was passing exams and passing them well. Me! I began to believe in myself a bit more. It took me another two years before I had the nerve to apply for a place on a degree course.

I was always in awe of people with degrees. I never dreamt that one day I would have one. When I decided to apply I was working as a student nurse. The decision to leave nursing was difficult especially as I was responsible for two children, but I knew that nursing wasn't for me. I was eventually accepted on a course through Mature Matriculation and the successful completion of an access course. This meant I had to attend college one day a week while still working as a nurse. The shifts made it difficult, but not impossible, and finally in September 1988 I left nursing and started on my degree course. My first day at college was one of the most frightening days in my life. I was so scared I could hardly walk. I couldn't believe it. Me on a degree course! Would I last the distance? Would I pass my finals? Oh God, what had I done?

By Christmas of the first term I was ready to leave. I'd just had an assignment returned which had what I regarded as a bad grade. I saw this as proof that I was too stupid to study for a degree and that I was a fool to think that I could do it. I went to see my personal tutor and somehow she talked me round. She tried to convince me that the grade wasn't so bad. In the end I grew bloodyminded enough to stay, determined not to let it beat me. In all truth I had no understanding of how to study for a degree, despite having studied recently. As amazing as it might sound I didn't understand what they meant when they said we should be reading. Reading what? I used to read my lecture notes! Eventually I did get the hang of it and began to settle down.

Looking back at my time at college I see it as an endurance test. It was sheer determination not to fail that kept me there. I felt as though I lurched from one panic to another, never really getting the full value of the opportunity. One of the things that made it so difficult was the travelling; on public transport, more often than not, it was a journey of one and a half hours, despite the fact that I only lived about ten miles from college. Fitting in study times was difficult too. Sometimes all I would have was an hour at night, once the kids had settled down. I was often exhausted. The pleasure that should go with being at college – the parties, boozy nights out, etc. – wasn't open to me. Running a house and raising children on a grant left no money for extras such as these. Practically, I would have been better off financially on Income Support, but spiritually I would have died.

Being at college was a difficult time, but it saved my life, and both saved and tested my sanity in many ways My confidence grew enormously. I was much more self assured, particularly after I had passed my first year exams and I knew that I would be returning. I met new friends who came to be very important to me. A lot of the mature students were also single parents. Strong, yet weak women. Strong in spirit, but weak in confidence. Determined to succeed despite . . . despite . . . always despite.

It was good to share the difficulties of coping with the many demands of college. I think that all of us, at various times, came close to quitting, but the others would rally round and provide the necessary support. Such strength and determination. Never underestimate the power of women!

Perhaps one of the most important things to happen to me at college was the increase in my political awareness. Through studying political perspectives I discovered a great deal about myself. Suddenly, feelings that I had thought were only particular to me, were found in books about feminist theories. A lot of my experiences and their effects were explained and validated. At times it was depressing to discover how widespread problems of abuse were, but ultimately, it was extremely satisfying to realise the amount being done by women to counteract such experiences. I felt the collective strength of women and was inspired. I felt as if I'd come home. I read books and thought 'Yes, me too. I feel that way too.' Suddenly I had labels to apply to things: 'patriarchy', 'radical feminism', 'socialist feminism', 'capitalism'. The things that are done to women in the name of patriarchy appal and anger me. I see no excuse for it. Men don't have to conform to their stereotypes. I refuse to conform to that assigned to women. But then, I haven't all that much power to lose.

I became angry at the attitudes of the right-wing factions of our society towards others, such as single parents, women and the working class – all of which applied to me. It angered me that people were labelled and often penalised financially and socially, irrespective of their individual circumstances. What did these people know about me and my circumstances, for instance? How dare they condemn me just because I fit into certain categories. I would like to see some of them live my life and be as successful!

One of the most difficult aspects to deal with is the poverty. The stress that comes from this is the worst because no end is in sight. It's not like the stress of having a high-powered job, because then a particular stress-causing project ends and you get your reward. Poverty just goes grindingly on, eroding all hope in its wake. One has to be very determined to stay afloat.

While a stronger, more confident me emerged during my time at college, I still retained aspects of the 'old' me. I still didn't like to believe that I would be successful. That was too much like tempting fate, in spite of my good grades, steadily improving from year to year. When my finals eventually came round I was resigned. I kept saying to myself, I can only do my best, no one can ask more than that. It was like a mantra.

I only had to wait three weeks for the results, but it seemed like a very long three weeks. I'll never forget the day they came. They arrived earlier than expected. When I saw the envelope I knew what it was immediately. I sat on the stairs with shaking hands and pounding heart and opened it. 'Please God, don't let me have failed.' I couldn't believe my eyes – I'd got a double first. Me! I really couldn't believe it. Only really intelligent people got firsts – not people like me. Once I had calmed down I realised the implications of it. This could open doors for me that had previously remained steadfastly shut. The power of a piece of paper! It allowed a working-class, single parent access to . . . I couldn't even begin to imagine what I now might be able to do.

My graduation day was very special to me. Having my

degree made me feel more like a worthwhile person. I realise that this should come from within, but this achievement allows me to believe in myself more. I'm not a complete failure – I can achieve things given the opportunity. It's being given the chance that is important.

One of the most important things that sustained me through-out my divorce and during the eleven years since, has been my friends and family. My mother helped me in practical ways, such as buying clothes for my children and taking us on holiday, and the emotional support from my childhood friend, Janet, kept me going. She is also a single parent. Our lives have been frighteningly similar, but this has given us a special bond that enables either one of us to support the other when needed.

It is only recently that I have come to understand and appreciate the value of knowing other women. I have started working with groups of women, and their unquestioned acceptance of me has done a great deal to improve my belief in myself as a capable, valuable human being. It has helped me to appreciate myself for what I have done, rather than as a reflection of someone else.

However, it is not quite that straightforward. The effects of the abuses I have suffered run very deep – so deep that they undermine everything I am. My whole personality has been shaped by my past experiences. No one facet of my life, or self, has escaped. Therapy has been painful and I have been through hell trying to come to terms with it all. It has made me question everything in my life – who I am, my relationship with my children, and my relationship to others. At this moment in time sex is abhorrent to me. I see it as a source of power wielded by men to control and subjugate me. It has nothing to do with love, more to do with dominance. Maybe I can overcome this as time goes by. I hope so.

I know I am a strong woman. I have coped with my

experiences in the best way I know. For the most part I coped on my own, and the price I paid was dear indeed. My children have also paid a price. My son recently asked about his father and wanted to see him. But his father has never been interested in seeing his children. Nevertheless I contacted him, something I was very loathe to do. He ignored my letter. I tried again. He ignored it again. It broke my heart to see my son hurting. I felt his pain. I wanted to erase it, but I couldn't. As for my daughter, she hides her feelings behind a hard, uncaring façade. She says she wouldn't care if her father dropped dead in front of her. I hate to think of the pain they must sometimes feel.

But it's not all bad. We are a family. We can please ourselves. The kids don't have to be on their best behaviour just in case their drunken father is in a bad mood. My daughter is sixteen years old and a beautiful person. I'm glad there is no male around oppressing her sexuality and her right to express it.

Past experiences have made me into the person I am today, for better or worse. Sometimes I feel very frightened and insecure, but I've also raised two lovely, caring children, successfully kept a household running and managed to obtain a first-class honours degree. Not bad for a frightened little woman who refused to give in and lay down and die!

I feel I am entering a new stage in my life – the 'me' stage. Probably for the first time in my life I am going to take my own needs and wants into consideration. I have denied myself for too long. I *am* a person of worth and I *deserve* to be taken notice of. I'm lucky though – I have a strong person on my side to help me when I falter. Me!!!

74

Wintergarden

Agnes Maria Burns

I am the fat narcissus bulb
still
completely covered in the dark soil.

April coming
and this will be my first
spring on earth.

All the past
was only preparation
the waiting and enduring
gathering the food
for my growth.

A VICTIM NO MORE

Frances Storey

'How are you all?'

It was the voice of my sister.

'Well, no one's crying, so I suppose we're all right'

We spoke for a while before the baby began his familiar, inconsolable crying which would last late into the night when, too tired to cry any more, he would finally sleep. I stole a few minutes to sit at peace and smoke a final cigarette before going to bed myself. This was the moment I most looked forward to, but the shortest lived, as, wrecked with exhaustion, I was instantly asleep.

I craved sleep and I craved peace. Each day began and ended with the crying of this beautiful, miserable child. The rejection I felt was so total it was as if I had been blotted out. I only existed in relation to my children, whose desperate need of me was overwhelming. Franny's solid world had fallen to pieces. Daddy was gone. In his place was this miserable baby, and me, crying, shouting, housebound, unloved and unloving. She did not recognise me and neither did I. How could I explain to a two-year-old what was happening when I did not understand myself? How could I love her when my nerves jangled and the baby's cries clawed at my mind, and all I could see was them – happy, loving and always, always laughing?

The demands of the day were terrifying. Could these three

half-crazed people make it till lunchtime without one of them finally going over the edge? Would the crying baby rest for more than ten minutes? Would the images of them together stop jumping out in front of me? I wanted to break down, give in. Anything for some peace. But I did not know how.

Separation is a slow and painful process. It is rarely final and never clean-cut. Each separate strand that joins you must be individually severed. You can hear it snap. The pain is physical. Each act of severance must be relived many times before the pain is dulled and you can look at the wound without crying.

It is only then that the healing can begin.

I could only measure time by the day. So one day at a time it was. Just one day at a time. At the end of that day, I would often look at my sleeping daughter, the sounds of my anger still hanging in the air, and tell her how much I loved her. I would stroke her cool skin and promise her that tomorrow would be better. I would try harder. I would somehow find time to read to her, to cuddle her and tickle her fat little tummy.

But it was too much for one person. And now, added to the pain of rejection, was a growing anger against him for taking away my ability to be the kind of parent I wanted to be. The kind of parent children need.

Those days can never be given back to Franny and Alex, can never be put right for them. I hated him for leaving me. For taking his love of life, his strength, his laughter and his great big heart away from us and giving them to someone else.

Many years later, Alex said to me, 'If I had been bigger, I would have pulled Daddy back as hard as I could to stop him from going away.'

You did your best, boy. You did your very best.

I was clear about the kind of person I did not want to be – the kind that clings and begs and whimpers. I could not let him see the desperation I felt, could not let him know how much I wanted him to stay. So I stood straight and alone and made him choose. He did not choose me.

I had read trite little articles about anger and how it can be a force for change. They made me feel more powerless than ever because I could not change the things I wanted to change. I could not make him come back. I could not make him want to be part of our family. I could not make the baby stop crying and, most of the time, I could not give Franny what she needed.

But then little unexpected things started to happen. I woke one morning to a silent house and for once my mind did not immediately spring into action, replaying yesterday's pain. I stretched out on the smooth, clean sheets. It felt good. It was my space. And for the first time I was glad that no one else was in that space. No one could touch me, tug at the covers or turn their shoulder away from me. It was my bed, not ours. It was mine and I liked it!

From that one feeling, the first moment of pleasure I had known since he left, things began to change. If I could enjoy this little patch of my life, then maybe I could extend the feeling. Maybe I had a right to be more than just a survivor. Suddenly I did not want to play the victim any more. I wanted some dignity, some fun, and, most of all, some control.

I could change some tiny bits of my life. I looked at the tinned milk which I used because he preferred it, and out of habit, had continued to buy. I preferred fresh milk. So I stepped outside to look for the milkman. He would deliver a pint a day starting tomorrow. We had a laugh and a joke. I felt ridiculously wonderful. The numbing routine soon dragged me down, but I hung on to that feeling of power.

I decided I wanted a daily paper, so I boldly walked into the newsagent and made the necessary arrangements. Easy! When my paper arrived the next morning, and I glanced through it while I sipped my coffee, topped with fresh milk, I felt drunk with the pleasure of it all.

78

I could change my name! Reclaim my old identity and discard one of the bonds between us. I was very excited about this idea. I made a mental list of all the people I would have to tell. Friends and family of course; the bank; people at my workplace; phone, gas and electric companies . . . Yes, this was a positive move. A clear decision.

I made some enquiries. Yes, you can change your name, but you can't change the names of the children without their father's permission.

I was stunned. I knew he would not agree and I did not want to ask because we were still trying to tear each other apart with every weapon we could lay our hands on. He would see this as a deliberate attempt to sever connections, not only with me, but with the children. And while I wanted to blame him for everything, show him all the damage he had done, make him feel guilt and regret, the last thing I wanted was for him to abandon us altogether. I was terrified of being totally responsible for the children, the house, the broken fence, the car. So I played a careful balancing act, pushing him as near to the edge as I dared, but always holding back the final, finalising words. I was later to be grateful for this restraint, even though my motives were suspect.

I was going to have to live without my own name.

Christmas was coming. The kids and I had survived for two whole months in our enclosed world full of tension and tears, but with increasing little patches of stillness as the baby slept a little more and cried a little less. The kind of stillness where love and pleasure can grow. Almost every day, someone arrived at the door bringing a plate of food, a bunch of flowers, a present for Franny. They would hold the crying baby for a while, play with his sister, and best of all, listen. I talked and talked: the latest transgression he had committed; the state of the kitchen floor; my innocence; my pain. I did not want to be cheered up. I did not want suggestions which might improve my life. Just let me be angry,

I wanted to say. Let me be mad. Let me cry. Get this weight off me.

They thought I was brave and strong. But it was they, those friends and family, who gave me strength. Without them . . . I cannot imagine.

I had managed to gather some Christmas presents together and to wrap them one December afternoon when Franny was out and the baby was sleeping. Then came the bombshell. He wanted to take Franny to the West Indies for Christmas to see his father. Would I agree? And why didn't I take Alex to Scotland to see my family? Take a plane. It would be all right. Franny would have a break. He would take me to the airport and collect me.

I did not want to do anything which might make him happy, like giving him his daughter for a week. The kids were my power, and I did not want to give half of that power away. But eventually, reluctantly, I agreed realising that we all needed a break, particularly Franny. She could have some fun for a change, and for me, one baby would be a rest. At the airport we kissed each other. A kiss filled with amazing sadness.

Alex was asleep in my arms. I hugged Franny and wondered if she would ever want to be with me again after a week of fun with her dad. She was the only person I actually wanted to spend Christmas with, and I was letting her go.

My family were shocked at my thinness, my drawn face and the fact that I had started smoking again. They were shocked at the miserable crying of the baby, and irritated. I was relieved to have some help, but very tense too, knowing he was ruining all the traditional Christmas events with his unending crying. I missed Franny badly. I was glad to get home.

On 24th Febuary I was supposed to return to work. I had no idea how it could all happen, given the demands of the children, and my exhaustion. I made plans for childcare, hoping they could somehow become a reality, but without much conviction. It was a complex patchwork, involving a child minder, baby sitters, their dad and minute timing. If it worked, I was released for very precise pieces of time to do my job. Once there, I was expected to be productive, energetic, innovative and caring. I felt none of those things, but the plan was in place. Maybe it could work.

The day finally came, and with it a culture shock. Life had been continuing as if nothing had happened. Gradually the plan became routine. I went thankfully to work where I found my old self still existed, the one that had a sense of humour, an interest in politics and films, and could even be good company. I was once again a person who enjoyed her job and had ideas.

I moved between two contrasting and demanding worlds. I arrived at work with baby dribbles on my shoulder and childish scribbles in my diary, a head full of worries (Had I remembered to put the washing on? Was I paying the childminder enough? How come everyone else could get the baby to sleep except me? And always, always, what was so great about her? Why did he choose her and not me? Why . . . ?)

I arrived home anxious about the pieces of work I had been unable to finish, mulling over some thorny problem, drained, desperate for sleep, but feeling more alive and part of life than I had for a long time. I felt very lucky to have a job that afforded me a reasonable income and a certain flexibility, and was also enjoyable. But I did feel extremely resentful that I was expected to do two full-time jobs alone.

He now had a place of his own where the children could stay overnight. We were full of hate and anger, but he was playing an increasing rôle in the children's lives, and that for me meant time, time on my own. At first that meant time to sleep, and then increasingly time to go out, shop, eat, read and meet the few friends I had left, having apparently lost most of them to him. So they preferred him too? Okay, time for me to be real, not one of a pair.

I took my first frightening peep at the future – my future. I looked beyond the next meal, the next demand on my energy. The picture was not too bright, but I did not panic. It looked bearable, even quite pleasant in bits. I felt better, at least, for being able to look. I looked around me with fresh eyes and saw clearly, for what seemed the first time, the house we had created together. I was shocked. How could I have chosen that wallpaper? Why had I agreed to buy that ghastly fire? That carpet? Had I given up on myself so much in the company of this large, fun-loving man?

Alex was almost a year old when, a little reluctantly, I made a trip to see some old friends. I had expected to be bolstered up with plenty of red wine and sympathy, but instead was put under what I considered undue pressure to do something. Do something? How can a victim do something? I felt angry with them for giving me another hurdle to jump. Hadn't I struggled enough? I drove slowly home, turning this idea over in my mind and realising that I was angry with them because I knew they were right. The circle could be broken, and I was the one who could break it.

I had one of my by-now-regular discussions with myself, putting both sides of the argument with amazing clarity. The subject was my son's first birthday party, which I had planned to use as another arrow with which to wound his dad, by excluding him. My debate ended with a narrow vote in favour of inviting him to share the day with us.

If relationships can turn on a single moment, then this was when it happened for us. He looked at me, slightly startled, then accepted. I had, in a single sentence, given him what he needed and what the children needed – the knowledge that he could have a real and unchallenged place in their lives. From that point on, we set about building a new kind of team and agreed rules – if largely unspoken.

We learned to talk without using words like weapons. He

would not let me sulk, I would not let him storm off. He would listen without diving for cover. The children became a focus, rather than instruments of war. I began to make choices based on what I wanted to do, not on what could hurt him the most.

The anger gradually loosened its grip. The downward spiral had been halted, had levelled off, and was heading into unknown territory. I was now convinced that I had to step out of the victim's rôle and into the unknown, if I was ever going to live in peace with myself, my children and their father.

During the following months, I learned more about myself than I had ever wanted to know. I was ruthless. Each new discovery was turned, examined, checked for truthfulness. I began to recognise where I stopped and the rest of the world began – a stage I had apparently missed out as a two-year-old. I claimed that person as me, acknowledged the feelings, the influences, the weaknesses. Particularly the weaknesses. And then, more slowly, the strengths. I had things to say, I had skills and, oh yes, I had faults. Having claimed all that as mine, I had no intention of falling apart – far from it. I was going to participate as an equal. Not as Prime Minister or as some kind of prize winner. Just as me.

This recognition and acceptance of myself took me, almost inevitably, to the next unimaginable step – to forgiveness. Of both him and of me. The kind of forgiveness that freed me from the anger, freed me to say 'Hello. How are you today?'; to put the happenings in our lives in context.

This was the journey I made in the months and years following his leaving. Painful, difficult and at times, tedious, this essential journey, from which there was no turning back, proved to be the key which released me.

It's a long, long road, and one I am still walking. But I know

I have become stronger and better equipped to live in this crazy world. A participant, not just an observer.

'What do you enjoy most about being alone?' My sister asked. After a moment I replied, 'Having a bed to myself.'

It is a real physical pleasure. My bed is still my haven, and no one can enter without an invitation, except my children who still regularly seek out the warmth and comfort it offers them. It is nice to have a little body to cuddle in the middle of the night sometimes. And it will not be long before they reject me in their fight for individuality.

My real adventure started as I stretched out on the smooth clean sheets alone. It is still the place where I feel safest and most at peace. There is no television or radio in my bedroom. I like it to be a quiet place with no distractions except books and my head.

I plan to be an outrageous old woman, full of wisdom and understanding, taking an active rôle in changing the world. I'll have plenty of spare beds and cupboards full of food to share. And I will enjoy my solitude too, because by then I will know just who I am. In the meantime, the struggle continues!

EVENSONG

Sun Sun Lwin

The only song I can sing
is my own

I learned it in my mother's body
its cadences and colours
distilled down through the
caverns and tunnels of her body
into my underwater world
the rhythms of ebb and flow
that sprang from her heart
rocked my liquid cradle

The song is mine now
new harmonies
from the patterns of my dreams
new rhythms
from my journeys of desire
new melodies
from my dancing thoughts

I hated my song for a long time
it seemed too thin and puny
a glass voice so clear and shrill
crying into emptiness
I wanted the full-bodied tones
of other tunes, rich and round
and ruby red like wine
So I hid my song and buried
my tongue in other melodies
I forgot my song so many times
and when I remembered that I had one
I could not easily find it
On searching I discovered that
pieces of it had stuck in my throat
like fishbones and glue
I had to wrench it out
I had to prise open my jaws
and pull out the song
all limp and bruised from neglect
from being crushed for so long
so pale from being kept in the dark

I wanted it then I wanted to sing
I was tired of other voices
I unfolded it and opened it out
It fell into shape filling out
each day a little more until
it spread across my life
into every corner from edge to edge

I sing my song every day now
and at night
I sing it in dreams

FUNNY HOW IT ALL TURNED OUT

Jane Cornwell

I'd always been a sucker for men who could make me laugh. When they were on stage doing it I think I laughed even harder – it's a kind of aphrodisiac, knowing that the guy who's up there making them all fall about will be sharing your bed afterwards.

Working as a waitress at a comedy venue in Melbourne I laughed a lot, but when a double act from London came to visit I pissed myself. I confessed to a girlfriend that I fancied the tall one, and she recommended that I move fast before he got 'snapped up'. Having just got back from a Latin American jaunt designed to help me overcome the break up of a five-year relationship I felt tanned, fit and supremely confident, so a swift move was no problem. Initially I think he found me a bit intimidating, declining an invitation for a game of pool, but at a club the next night he presented me with a poem he'd written especially and I couldn't get him into a taxi fast enough.

It was an Australian summer of love, a mixture of all the right ingredients: sex, drugs, drink, rock 'n' roll, midnight swims and good conversation, with a helluva lot of reflected glory thrown in. My stature increased amongst my peers and I marvelled at his endless tales of fame and fortune in a land then far enough away to seem almost mystical. He told me how he got recognised wherever he went, occasionally mobbed by schoolchildren (he'd compered a Saturday morning TV show), of how he'd started out as a street performer earning virtually nothing and become a six-figure media celebrity. I admired his allegiance to the street and was readily introduced to the like of Kerouac, Hemingway and Rimbaud, Jack Daniels, bull fighting and descriptive prose. He told me he'd slept with over sixty women, that back home he had five regular girlfriends, some of whom valued him for his 'mind', others for what he did 'in bed'. He proclaimed himself a confirmed bachelor – a hard-drinking, hard-smoking, hard-living kinda guy who named several rock stars as drinking buddies and considered breakfast to be for wimps.

It all went very fast and within a short period of time we were both completely and totally in love. I had a full-time job at the Royal Melbourne Institute of Technology and was attempting to do an MA part time, as well as work at my beloved comedy venue, and very soon that all suffered. I couldn't be without him. I hadn't felt that way for years. I was on a kind of perpetual high which made the sun shine brighter and the sky seem bluer. I felt attractive, sexy, intelligent and lusted after. Making love took me to realms of ecstasy never previously imagined. One very stoned night he traced 'I love you' on the palm of my hand and it was as if the Universe had stopped just for that moment. The poetry flowed, I was his muse, his inspiration, his *raison d'être*. I guess I overlooked a lot. I wanted to keep him as that figure on stage that everyone wanted to get close to. When he rode in the car boot on late night drives to the beach or had to run off to throw up during yet another ferocious hangover, I thought him whacky and wild. When he drunkenly looked up my flatmate's dress as she stepped over him or flirted outrageously with other women at parties, I thought him untamed and challenging. That he rarely bathed and his socks just about walked around the room by themselves fed my image of him as a kind of Bohemian Jack-the-Lad.

When it was time for him to go, part of me was actually relieved – two months of solid partying had begun to take their toll and I looked forward to some personal space again. I was also exhausted from weeks of playing a rôle, in which I too was a hard-living sexual being who burnt the candle at both ends, eschewed social convention and lived for the moment – a part he'd written and for which I could have received an Oscar nomination.

After he left I missed him, but not excessively so. In keeping with the character I'd been playing I'd deliberately not pressed him about any future developments, careful to keep to his maxim that we were both 'free spirits'. Underneath the façade, however, my gut feeling told me that if I played my cards right it wouldn't be long before his bachelor pad was retitled by my presence. Sure enough, the letters, phonecalls and flowers came thick and fast. My flatmate would laugh uproariously at some of the things he'd write (do men actually realise how much women share?); he'd elevated me to an almost goddess-like position that she – and I, in my more sane moments – found hilarious. It's easy to hide your faults from someone you know is leaving shortly. So, when he told me he couldn't live without me and that a plane ticket was on the way, it came as no surprise. I left career, family and friends and flew 12,000 miles to reside in a land where I knew no one but him.

The honeymoon period lasted a few months, as I desperately avoided slipping off the pedestal. Whether my imagination had been overactive or I'd basically succumbed to bullshit I'm not sure, but nothing seemed as grand or impressive as it had done long distance. His flat was tiny, his media connections tenuous, and I found London dirty and oppressive. I was paraded before the volleyball team, the 'boys' from the pub and the comedy circuit and did my best to believe the hype. A couple of times he cried because he loved me so much.

The flat was always a mess. I remember reading letters from

old girlfriends he'd left lying around ('I've got no secrets from you' he used to say) and thinking that they couldn't be directed at the man I knew. Lying? Alcoholism? Trying to cut his wrists? Verbal bombardments? Well, I thought, they've obviously just been the wrong women. He wouldn't do any of that to me. After all, he'd said he'd never hurt me.

The TV audience is a fickle beast, and his career took a downhill turn. Dropped from the box he went back to performing live, paying for me to accompany him and his partner on national tours. The fights had started, as I, increasingly homesick, began to see through the bravado. In Australia I'd had a lot of friends, a promising writing career and an academic future; I think we'd both assumed I'd be able to duplicate this in England. I embarked on a series of menial jobs, unable to find 'decent' work, and arguments about money became monotonous in their regularity. The TV was always on, from the moment he woke up till the wee hours of the night, and I began to have headaches as frequent as the financial disagreements. Without employment I found it difficult to make friends. He encouraged me to pursue links he'd forged for me but my self-esteem was continually at a low ebb and my confidence, once so attractive in its brashness, was pretty much cracked. The relationship became my whole life, and this led to resentment on both sides. No longer was I the strong, independent woman of a few months previous. And what had seemed so impossible in the ex's letters–the constant drinking, verbal abuse, compulsive lying and infidelities – was now exemplified at every opportunity. I am a gamut of double messages: one moment, 'I love you and want to spend the rest of my life with you'; the next, 'You've got one more chance you selfish, useless bitch.' The dividing line between what was acceptable and what was unacceptable became increasingly blurred.

I got pregnant during the Edinburgh Festival. He had an affair just after the abortion. The enormity of it all was just too much for him to cope with and, while he liked to have his girlfriend around all the time, his insecure performer's ego constantly sought affirmation elsewhere. He'd tell me he was 'just out to feed the ducks' and off he'd go to meet some girl. I know because the level of distrust I felt was so intense I'd search his clothes for evidence, hating myself for doing it but hating him even more when I did find something.

I began to assume guilt readily and easily, to believe the labels he plastered me with: that I was crazy, stupid, demanding, a loser, that I needed help. That it was my fault I was lonely and miserable, that I didn't know what I wanted. I knew I had become addicted to the relationship and I wanted to leave but couldn't. Perhaps in Australia it might have been different – I had relinquished so much power by coming to London. I'd stopped liking him a long time before, but the love and hate I felt were equally intense. I guess it was the same for him too.

It must be hard being well known one day and a nothing the next. He'd had his fifteen minutes when we started seeing each other, yet I was led to believe I'd be living the lifestyle of the rich and famous. I remember a particularly bad dose of 'flu after the electricity had been cut off, when I seriously considered suicide. I couldn't get any kind of clarity in my thinking; I felt mentally trapped even though he would have been glad if I had walked out the door way before I did. Many, many times he'd stick his face half an inch away from mine (the personification of evil when drunk), with eyes narrowed to slits and spittle coming out his mouth, and go on and on with barrages of verbal abuse. Once a lucid, spunky woman, I'd cringe and let the tension creep up my body until I felt I'd explode.

After two years of highs (when I felt I would burst because I loved him so much) and lows (when I became a shaking, sobbing nervous wreck), a mutual friend came over. I told her that things weren't too good (we'd presented a happy face to the world); how he'd head-butted me when I tried to block his way and then told me it was my fault for moving forward; how desperate and alone I felt. She acted swiftly and decisively, something I'd forgotten how to do. 'Right,' she said. 'Take deep breaths – we're moving you out. Is this yours? This?' And so on until I ended up at her place.

I really only wanted to give him a shock. Earlier on he had cried when I had threatened to leave him, and told me our relationship was the most important thing in his life. How the tables had turned! Now he wanted me out, unless I promised to change.

So I tried to go back. He let me at first, with a whole long list of provisos which I knew I could never fulfil. 'No more headaches' was one of them. One day I started weeping at the stupidity of it all. He exploded and told me to get out of his life. I begged him to see reason, prompting a drunken diatribe which led to physical violence on both sides. We thought my arm had been broken and he tried to drag me to the hospital. But I broke free and ran off to where I'd been staying.

Still I tried to go back. I felt lost, desperate, with nothing to lose, My dignity had flown out the window and my pride had gone with it. I'd turned myself into a complete victim. I rang him constantly. The worst thing he said was 'Just go away,' and once I nearly got run over as I ran across the road to get to him.

About two weeks after the breakup he finally relented and agreed to meet for a drink. But when I rang at his door there was no answer. So, like someone possessed, I stood on the street corner until I finally saw him going up the steps with his arm around a woman. I turned and ran. That for me was the moment I really hit rock bottom; the point when I said to myself that enough was enough.

My recovery wasn't easy. My main dilemma was whether to tough it out in London or run back to Australia, and I decided to opt for the former. In the past I had relied on friends and family to help pull me through crises, or packed up and gone on extended travels to block out my feelings with new sights and adventures. This time I decided to face my demons head on, and I explored many different avenues in an attempt to find and love myself again.

I made my first priority to cut all contact with him, to rediscover that iron will I knew was lying dormant. No matter how much I wanted to phone or write, I didn't let myself – I knew it would only impede my recovery. I phoned every woman I'd had some sort of connection with and probably bored a lot of them silly as I endlessly recounted my tale of woe, hoping to establish a small support network. Some were wonderful, others quite dismissive, but what did I expect from people I hardly knew? I steeled myself to a routine, bought some vitamins and made myself eat when just the thought of food was enough to make me retch. I kept an eye on my coffee and cigarette intake and vowed to do something nice for myself each day.

When you break up with someone so traumatically, you notice all the seemingly happy couples. Was I the only single woman in London? And the saccharin lyrics of love songs really tug at the heartstrings. I searched for some uplifting music, and thought of putting together a compilation with the likes of 'I Will Survive' and 'Sisters Are Doing It For Themselves'. I stopped drinking alcohol and smoking dope, as both clouded my mind and obscured my thinking.

I devoured self-help books – *Women Who Love Too Much*, *Men Who Hate Women and the Women Who Love Them*, *Good Men, Bad Men and Other Lovers*, *Love Shock*, *Creative Visualisation*, *You Can Heal Your Life* – and a regular plethora of other titles. From each I drew what I thought most relevant to me and most helpful to my recovery. I needed to piece together my shattered self-esteem and eradicate the thought that I was truly unlovable, as I had let myself believe. I did endless exercises such as gazing into a mirror and repeating

'I approve of myself' and 'I love you' until it became more enervating than embarrassing.

I recognised some of the various pitfalls, such as the danger of magnifying what I thought he was doing. It didn't matter anyway, I'd tell myself – he was completely out of my life. I learned to turn a negative into a positive, to counterbalance a desperate thought with a rational response on paper. Writing it all down helped the most. I kept a diary with me at all times and wrote prolifically about my fears and doubts, and reiterated that the relationship was truly over. Until I totally acknowledged that I don't think my recovery had truly begun. I even considered making a tape outlining why it was destructive and why it had to finish, and playing it on my Walkman.

I began to change my behaviour. I knew that the good feelings would catch up, and I didn't want to feel that way ever again. I threw things out that reminded me of us: I had a little ritual burning of the reams of poetry; I stashed the photos away. I wrote down all the things I'd given up for the relationship, began to reassess my goals and aspirations, beliefs and opinions, and what I really wanted from a relationship.

I learned to get straight out of bed when I woke up to stop me lying there and thinking of him. I kept going to my mundane job and writing furiously when it all became too much. I set aside fifteen minutes twice a day to scream and cry and beat a pillow – what I called my 'allocated grieving time.' I wrote down the good and bad things about the relationship and him and was astounded at the weight of the latter. I learned to appreciate simple things, like the smile of a child, a walk in the park, a flower in bloom. I learned that if I felt awful today, perhaps I wouldn't feel the same way tomorrow, and I certainly wouldn't feel this way forever. I began to like myself again.

One of the books said that you go through various stages after a breakup: shock, grief, blame (self-blame or otherwise), resolution and rebuilding, and you can get stuck in one or sway between two for a while. I went through them all, perhaps staying in the blame stage a bit too long, and have now completely disempowered him through forgiveness. This was one of the hardest things to do, but now, nearly two years down the track, I can wish him the best. I hear *about* him from time to time but have no desire to contact him. Too much damage was done for us to be friends.

Slowly things started coming together. I have a good job, many friends and interests. I tried the one-night stand bit for a little while but decided it wasn't for me. I've had a couple of relationships but feel that I need to be single until I really know myself well enough to enter a fulfilling relationship. I can also see straight through the crap these days, which limits my options a bit. I've made a regular commitment to therapy and consider it one of the best things I've ever done, although it's often a painful journey towards finding myself, knowing who I am and what I want. I still like men who make me laugh – preferably offstage – but for the time being I'm content to enjoy my own company, that of my friends', and life's rich tapestry. And I haven't had a headache in a long, long time.

LET US LEAVE THEM BELIEVING

Katie Campbell

Let us pretend we are lovers again
just once for this visit
to friends who thought we were perfect together
for all the love and the envy
they wasted on you and me
let us leave them believing.

SEPARATE LIVES

Margot Francis

Can this really be part of the process? The wild rushing round
the house, looking for the invitation from Hollywood in the
post, making up unnecessary fires, cleaning the inside of a cup
with intense concentration – alternating with falling asleep at
the desk at noon?

Yes, it's completely familiar.

So what am I avoiding writing this time?

A three-thousand-word article on divorce.

Ah, why?

Because I don't know where to begin and I'm afraid of
bloodying my hands.

Who can live in this world with clean hands? To talk about
the middle you have to start near the beginning. Go back, I
tell her, my younger self, as Dorothy Whipple told hers, in
The Other Day.

Couldn't you tell another story?

No, it has to be this one. It's time. Go back.

I watch unblinking as she twists and turns and dwindles
down the years.

I am seven years old. My father has been ill in bed for some
days. Then this day, the 21st March 1946, my mother calls me
in from playing and says, 'Kneel down and pray to God not

to let your daddy die.' I do and he does. In five minutes my desperate mother had brought a budding relationship with the old man and his white beard to an abrupt end and had made me feel responsible for my father's death: obviously, in the eyes of those who mattered, I wasn't good enough to save him.

These two consequences affected my future life in important ways. But the death of my father also resulted in my having to become my depressed mother's husband (no wonder my shoulders bowed and buckled), in an unnaturally tight bonding that idealised the dead male.

In addition, the absence of my father and of any other man in my life, I now see, with the help of Linda Schierse Leonard's *The Wounded Woman*, contributed to the very low self-esteem, the lack of confidence in my ability to work in the world from which I suffered for years, and to the difficulty I had in committing myself to trust in lasting relationships. After all, if the first woman in my life was threatening to gobble me up, the first man had abandoned me. Fierce control and lack of playfulness became features of my psychological landscape. Encased in that Amazonian armour as I grew up, I found it increasingly difficult to embrace my feminine identity and my sexuality. Instead, I blocked this energy off in my gut, together with all the unspent rages and the unshed tears.

So God the Father had gone. My personal father, who might have encouraged me, provided me with a model for success, direction, discipline, had gone. Who *were* men? What were they like? What did they do? Did they joke, sweat, feel the same things, ever? Only the patriarchs of my culture, with their distorted and devalued projections of the feminine, were left to answer.

All unconscious of this rich and complex psychological background, I met the man who was to become my first husband.

We were reading – or 'doing', as I used to say – English in the same year at university. My first impression of him was that he looked like one of Thurber's dogs. But there was a tantalising air of maturity about him, for he had completed National Service, he wasn't another of your pink-cheeked schoolboys. He was tall and quickwitted and we had stimulating sessions of word play. He was gregarious and introduced me to some interesting people who were his friends.

Although I was engaged to an older man who was, yes, an engineer like my father, and he, Robert, was also engaged to a teacher, we started going out together in an innocent sort of way – an outing to Stratford with fellow students, trips to the theatre, a European drama tour when we were fellow-actors in the same dire production.

On the first day of term in our second year, when I was twenty, had broken off my engagement (whatever did it mean? what *was* marriage?) and had arranged to share a house in West London with three other women students, he met me at Euston station to tell me it was all over. I was sunk in misery and he vacillated. We became 'lovers' at the house a few weeks later.

I had been deflowered by hand by my fiancé near Symond's Yat, but my first taste of intercourse was with Robert, over the end of a sofa in the living room, fully clad except for pants, one Saturday evening when all the others were out. Bitter it was: no emotion, no technique, no foreplay involving breast or clitoris (the clitoris wasn't invented for me till 1980) – and *coitus interruptus.**

I had received very confused messages from my mother about sex, marriage, men, children, work . . . especially sex. It was apparently wonderful, but the mark of a sinful immoral nature to indulge in it before marriage. My diaries of those

* I hereby propose, throughout the country, Schools of Love, to be staffed by older women, who would teach the arts of love to young women and men, thus ending the years of misery and ignorance an awful lot of people have suffered.

years make very sad, very punitive, reading. But if we weren't using a Durex, the activity wasn't taking place, was it?

A few weeks after Robert and I had this first and no doubt other scarcely more enjoyable experiences, we four women decided to hold a party. Robert was invited and had indeed insisted on inviting several other guests of his choice, but he wasn't much in evidence. At one point I looked casually out of the front window and there he was, talking to one of the sirens of the English year below ours.

As our relationship (I won't say courtship) staggered on over ten years, this emotional/sexual betrayal was part of the pattern. He couldn't commit himself and I hadn't the self-esteem, the confidence, the raging guts, to walk out. Love didn't come into it, but the lurching familiarity of abandonment did.

It was sado-masochistic, I realised later; he the sadist, I the masochist – we fitted like a glove a hand. That's why I bought him lunches and paid him to give me (a few) driving lessons. (He was curiously mean with money.) That's why I didn't walk out in 1964 when I thought I was pregnant and he said he didn't want to marry me, why didn't I get an abortion? (I wasn't pregnant and have never had a child.) That's why I colluded in some of his sexual games – for instance, exposure. Ironically, my mother's favourite adjective for Robert was 'wholesome'. Our sex life never improved, but I didn't seem able to get my being round the concept that it could be/should be fulfilling, enjoyable, arousing, amusing – all those things.

We met in 1957, married in 1967 – and of course we shouldn't have done it. We married in the end because of social pressures. Our three parents were puzzled by our ten-year relationship and our friends were all married or marrying. I remember, a short while before the wedding, transporting my goods and chattels from London in a van and crying the whole way.

On our honeymoon, in south-west Spain, he had crabs –

pubic lice – and we didn't make love. Four years later we went back to the same place and I came down with food poisoning. Again we didn't make love – there was none to make. In between, he had an affair – our friends thought – with someone at work. She was a widow with a small son. He certainly brought her to the house often and we all spent Christmas together one year. He used work as an excuse not to meet with me, not to talk with me. The subject of having children was never addressed, for instance, though he later rebuked me for our not having any. We were both working full time, but I'd been got at by the patriarchs and their female helpmeets to expect to have to undertake two jobs and I spent most Saturdays brushing, waxing, polishing the wooden floors of our so-called labour-saving bungalow. I also remember meeting Robert walking down a street in the town where we both worked one lunch-time, with a male crony. They were talking and laughing, on their way to the pub for a pint. I was the human gorilla, weighed down by two pendulous bags from M&S, full of comestibles to feed his friends that weekend. I loathed him then; I burned with resentment.

Shortly after our second trip to Spain, he became depressed, then left. We hardly talked at all about what was wrong; certainly not with any illumination. Abandoned, I was shocked and cried a lot. He said he thought that was what I wanted. He was right, but it took me years to face up to my responsibility in the matter, to stop playing victim. He wanted to try again after a while, but by that time I had become entangled with the man who was to become my second husband.

I met Charles at the publishing house where we both worked. Soon after Robert left me he, unknowing, began to seek me out. I confided in him and we began an affair quite quickly, though he was married for the second time (again with no children). I didn't fancy Charles. Physically, then, he was a figure of fun: he had long, dark greasy hair, an absurdly long, shiny and rubbed overcoat, which he wore with a scarf forever trailing. Gloves he forbore, because he left them everywhere.

He left women everywhere too. He warned me before we started living together in 1973, that he only wanted, perhaps, to pick the pretty flowers, but I arrogantly thought I could change him. I couldn't. He couldn't trust long-term commitments either, though we married in 1975 and at first he wanted children. Our most popular dance was one of control and evasion. Something feminine in Charles appreciated my Amazonian control, but he always slipped out from under and, as a refinement, tried to let me know he was doing so. For instance, the initial excitement we had sexually faded as it does – especially where there's no technique or knowledge, only an overriding anxiety about premature ejaculation. Charles went to a 'house' in Soho which showed blue films. He made sure, while denying it, that I saw the membership card he'd written out in his hand but with a mutual friend's name and address.

Another area of difficulty was that he and my mother heartily disliked and were both jealous of the other. I felt torn in half.

Despite these minuses, I gradually grew to love Charles and felt calm and happy on our wedding day. We had a lot in common: he was another English graduate, but with a finer sensibility than Robert. He wrote good poetry and his views on literature and the arts in particular always stimulated me, even when I disagreed. He was supportive of me at work. We quickly grew to like most of each other's friends and were happy exploring the countryside near our cottage.

After four years of marriage the balance of power in our relationship was shifting: he was standing out against my control. Then fate intervened: our mothers, to whom we were both ambivalently attached, died within two months of each other. In our great grief, mine expressed, his suppressed, neither could help the other, give comfort. He turned to his secretary, and I to depression, restless journeys, suicidal thoughts – and my clitoris. After betrayals on both sides, I finally left him in 1983, though we had lived together more or less as friends for the last two years.

Both Charles and Robert divorced me without discussion, and each time I received those papers, each time I heard they'd married again, I felt a pang: strange familiars, familiar strangers. I see Charles for lunch, we are friends, and I still feel love for him, even knowing all his weaknesses; still dream regularly of him with other women. Robert has become meaner, imperious, malicious, touchy – especially with feminist women – so there's nothing left, no point in meeting.

Looking back at them, my two husbands, and at my young woman self, what do I see? I perceive at last my main pattern. I chose two men – one who tried to control me, the other whom I tried to control – both Don Juans with ambivalent feelings about their mothers and women, who are probably bisexual, i.e. repressed homosexuals. Two men who were very likely to abandon me in that exquisitely painful and deliciously familiar way my father did. (He was, I think, having an affair at the time of his death and my mother invited his mistress, but not me, to his funeral.) To abandon me, thus permitting me to indulge, as my mother and I had done, in pathological mourning and a prolonged sense of victimisation.

And looking into the mirror now, at myself in my waning moon phase, what do I see? How have I survived? How am I different? How far have I travelled through the labyrinth?

I can begin to answer these questions by examining my relationship with the significant other in my life now. I live with a younger man, whom I also met through work. He's loving, non-critical and has been extremely supportive of me. We struggle together over our temperamental differences, our

103

individual *idées fixes*, to transform. We are not happy all the time by any means. He teaches me about the physical world, the world of nature and the body; I teach him about the psychological world, the world of psyche and the Self. We have separate work and rooms to do it in; we sleep separately sometimes. We each travel for our work, go out with our individual friends in the evening, or to night school; to some extent – though not sexually – lead separate lives. We are striving to be equal partners, to examine stereotypical attitudes, to really communicate through the pain, and to let go. Although we have known sexual ecstasy – including orgasm for me, too, at last – during our twelve-year relationship, we no longer have penetrative intercourse. This is partly because as a post-menopausal woman I have vaginal dryness and do not want to risk HRT; partly for psychological reasons. I am now able to tell my lover when what he's doing is pleasurable and when it is not, to ask for what I want. I believe I am more open and adventurous than he is, sexually.

How have I survived? I've come through a lot – the death of my family, two divorces, the menopause and a long period of grieving, unemployment and non-recognition of my work. Suffering has taught me, refined me. I have also worked hard on my personal development by attending workshops, having psychotherapy over three and a half years, behavioural therapy over ten weeks and acupuncture most recently, which has literally put me in touch with the block in my guts, my 'dead centre'. I cracked open at my mother's death, closely followed by the breakdown in my second marriage, and began to change and develop: I started slowly to trust myself and my intuitions, to gradually have faith in my skills and talents, potential and progress.

After twenty years in publishing, I also got round the other side of the desk and began to write – stories, journalism and plays for all media. I've had to serve a long apprenticeship, but after several years' committed work and a hail of rejection slips

I am beginning to sell my work, be published, have rehearsed readings, be encouraged and accepted. This has increased my self-esteem and confidence, and the path at last is spiralling upwards.

The writing has fed into the psycho-spiritual development too, of course. I can trace this clearly. Although in my psycho-therapy we did not seem to address the wound of my father's death, nor did I feel I was offered good enough mothering at last, the therapist did offer me myth and thus started me on the Jungian royal road to individuation. I was encouraged to read about Eros and Psyche in Apuleius' *Golden Ass*. Clusters of symbols began to form some time afterwards, including first butterflies (Psyche-transformation), then bees (the matriarchy), snakes (the Goddess), labyrinth (overcome death at the centre), moon and stars (Artemis-Diana), and now the Grail (regeneration). I have written a short story called 'Butterflies', which has just won a prize, a screenplay framed by passages from Maeterlinck's *The Life of the Bee*, a long story set in Crete, and a play for the stage about Artemisia Gentileschi. This process has taken years and has been punctuated by volcanic rages (the Goddess Kali regularly manifested in my kitchen), violence, and tears – all symptoms of my healing, which my partner has been able to accept.

Artemis, among many other attributes, is complete in herself, i.e. virgin, and has brought into my life a sense of my own independence and empowerment, the urge to live in and through my body at last and to come to terms with wild things, since she is Lady of them. These are without – I've always been nervous of animals – and within – my sexuality and non-rational playfulness and spontaneity.

These qualities, resulting from changes in my psyche at a profound level, have become my deep needs, desires and ideals. It is essential now for me to have long periods of solitude and silence, with as much freedom from restriction as possible. I couldn't have stayed confined in coupledom in those marriages, with no name of my own, no life of my own, no Self of my own; with men so insecure, so unknowing of themselves, so unwilling to develop and change. My partner and I will not marry. Although my head recognises marriage's current legal, social, religious and economic implications, my heart and my guts still don't know what it bestows that cohabitation doesn't, and are repelled by the psychological and emotional concept of becoming one flesh.

I have begun to learn through all the suffering what I am, what I can do and what I am not interested in doing. I have learned that there is no security except in your Self. I am determined, for as long as I live, to go on developing, trying to change, striving to achieve equality; to climb with other women onto the main stages of the cultural and political institutions of this country.

CHAOS THEORY

Diana Barber

Chaos Theory: Snowflakes are a good example
Self-similar systems reproducing
within the same circle of space
Tree branches frame windows we look through
into endless self-similar systems

I hate the calculating edges of snowflakes
Your snowflakes
You sit on my back like a snowflake and I turn
to my cold point of reference
repeating the pattern in circles of space
Too late I missed it you melted
years ago

Trees are not responsible!
Snowflakes shape nothing on the world except beauty
and Beauty (they told me I listened)
is in the eye of the beholder
In my eyes are dead wood and melted water
You are my fierce gladness
my glad to have met you
this time I refuse to regret
I will accept only that
I am glad to have met you

LEAVE MY CHICKENS ALONE!

Sue Thomas

My parents taught me that a married couple should never air their differences in public. That they should always present a united face to the world.

Well, I tried.

Meet my husband – he has an emotional age of three, but I agree with everything he does.

Meet my husband – the only person he's interested in is himself, but I agree with everything he says.

Meet my husband – he's a tedious bore, but oh, no! he never bores me!

How long can you do that? I did it for fourteen years and two children.

I never left the room when he talked about himself to our dinner guests for hours on end.

I never walked away when he lost his temper and shouted curses at me in the street.

And when he stomped off in a rage, I collected up the kids and followed on behind.

When he said we wouldn't go somewhere, we didn't go.

When he proclaimed that it was bourgeois to enjoy buying things new instead of secondhand, or that talking about literature is pseudo-intellectualism – I agreed.

He suffered, you see. He was tortured. He couldn't help it,

and he usually apologised afterwards. Naturally, he knew it wasn't a good idea to lock himself in his room for three days at a time, or to punch holes in doors with his fist. But he just couldn't help it. Sometimes he'd cry with remorse afterwards and I'd hold him in my arms and say don't worry, I know you didn't mean it.

Of course, now I understand where I went wrong. My mistake was that I believed you can change people if you work hard enough. But how can you change someone whose childhood was pampered and indulged? I married a little boy of twelve who refused to open his Christmas presents until New Year's Day, just to spite his over-bearing mother. A child of eight who spent his days hiding in a tree to spy on the other children instead of joining them in a game. A man of twenty subject to such rages that he would shake with uncontrollable fury at a spot of paint spilled on a table.

I thought I could help him, you see. He just needed to know he was loved and cared for and everything would be all right.

Fantasy.

It was my fantasy that he would look after me when I became pregnant for the first time. Instead, he resented my tentative bids for attention. (I'd seen them on the telly, these loving men who delight over the blossoming mother-to-be. They do exist. Since then I've even met one or two.)

It was fantasy that he would spend hours buying my birthday present, like I did with his. In reality, birthdays and Christmas generally provoked a row followed by some item sullenly presented. And it was certainly fantasy that he would ever enjoy doing things for the children.

And sex? That was *his* fantasy, mostly to do with men's magazines. As for me – he said I had a body like a tub of lard.

Well, Reader, I chucked him out. It took fourteen years to work up to it, but once I made up my mind there was no going back.

After he left, the house exploded with colour and I fell in love for the first time.

My husband had been slowly renovating our large Edwardian house for the past five years. It was now completely undecorated, with bare plaster everywhere. On my first evening alone I painted the kitchen notice-board red and yellow. My first creative act! In the year that followed I decorated every room in the house in strong, bright colours.

I spent much of that year in the company of my first real lover. I had never before known such tenderness with another human being; when we were apart it truly felt as if I was missing a limb of my own body. I loved him very much, but it was easy to forget how emotionally raw I was. As every other area of my life brightened and grew, I poured all my anxieties into that relationship until it soured and was spoiled. It ended slowly and painfully, but I look back on it with gladness, because at least now I can say I know what it is to really want someone with every fibre of your being. I've never had such an intense experience before or since. No doubt the whole thing was heightened by the circumstances; so was it ever True Love? I'll never know.

I had other relationships too, and I learned a lot about people in the first couple of years. I also rediscovered a lot about myself. I went back in time to my teenage years, when the world was strange and new. I played Joni Mitchell and Nina Simone, read Dylan Thomas and thought again about poetry. In my teens I'd always wanted to be a writer – I had a fantasy of sitting at a desk beside a pair of french windows, composing novels while my children played happily on the sunlit lawn outside. Well, I'd got the kids and the french windows but the novels remained out of reach.

But other things were simmering away nearer the surface, and practical matters came high on my agenda.

After the separation my husband agreed to sign his half of the house over to me in lieu of maintenance. We both knew that he would be highly unlikely to keep up any regular payments to me – he had never earned much and he'd left his job and gone back to live with his parents within weeks of our splitting up. I signed on and received roughly enough to keep us and pay the mortgage interest. We'd always lived quite frugally, and I took a lodger to help out. But I had no intention of staying at home forever, so when the autumn arrived I signed on for a couple of courses at the local FE college.

In the past I'd been able to earn a little money with my knitting machine, so it seemed a good idea to study textiles further. Also, just out of interest, I thought I'd have a go at 'A' level English. It proved to be the most exciting thing I'd done in years, and by the following September I had got myself a place on a Humanities BA course at my local Polytechnic.

The Poly was hard at first. The girls were six and eight when I started my degree. I had no car, and toiled up and down a windy hill to college throughout the winter. Sometimes I had to take the kids to lectures, where they were unbelievably well-behaved. By the first Christmas my hectic love-life had ground to a halt and I was spending all my time at home studying.

And there were other targets still to be met. I decided to kill two birds with one stone by giving up smoking to pay for driving lessons and an ancient car. I still don't know whether it was nicotine withdrawal or studying, but I became very introverted that winter and found it difficult to communicate with my friends. It was at that time that I started to hide myself away. After two years of a busy social life my priorities had changed and I became pretty self-centred and probably quite unpleasant to be with, but it seemed necessary just to concentrate on my studies and home life.

By the summer I'd passed my driving test and started smoking again (much to everyone's relief, I think!). But I'd also discovered another priority to be pursued.

Priorities have led me by the nose for quite some time now.

111

I always have something to work towards. In fact, I've become an obsessive planner, frustrated by the loss of fourteen years of my life. There are so many things I haven't done and there *must* be a way to fit them all in.

The next priority was to learn about computing. Curiosity had led me to study a short course in Information Technology, and it wasn't long before I was hooked. Because control is essential to my life – there are so many strands holding it together – I became quite fascinated by the nature of machines. If only human behaviour were predictable, and if our faults could be reprogrammed into perfection, then think how safe our lives would be! I wrote my final year dissertation about computers, and still think and write about them now.

Well, time went on. I studied. Lodgers came and went. The girls grew up. For the three years I was at college our large semi housed a stream of friends, lodgers, children – and conversation. At times it all got too much. The girls and I were sometimes frustrated by the lack of peace and quiet, but there were benefits too. Most of our lodgers were female (the two men we had didn't work out at all) and the girls formed close friendships with several of them. We acquired two dogs – and chickens.

Within six months of the separation I had built a hen-house and bought some birds, and we continued to keep hens for the next four years until we moved house. I've always been fond of chickens – one of my earliest memories is of collecting the eggs from the warm-smelling straw of a relative's poultry house. But after the separation the hens became important in another, more mystical way.

I began to dream about chickens! They seemed somehow to represent my spiritual and intellectual freedom, and hens featured in a series of dreams, especially after the barren time following my father's death. At that time, for example, I dreamed I'd found a cold and starving hen in the yard.

'I've been here all the time,' it said, 'You just forgot about me.' I picked it up, brought it into the house and warmed it in my lap.

Several times, when things were going badly in the real world, I embraced these cold dream-hens and revived them. Once I even dreamt that my husband and I decided to get back together, whereupon he said I would no longer need my hens. In the dream he set the hen-house alight and tried to burn my birds alive. Of course, I couldn't go back with him after that. Some people have suggested that these chickens are my spirit guides, and that seems to make sense.

However, flesh-and-blood poultry in the suburbs are easy prey for the urban fox, and I lost several flocks before reluctantly giving them up. I'll get them back one day.

But we still have the dogs. Companions and guards, they make us safe and we love them very much. I feel it's important for the children of single-parent families, and also those children who have to adapt to a second marriage, to have a pet to cuddle when they feel alone and ignored.

The biggest problems with my kids arose in those early years when I was too involved with myself to spend as much time as I should have done thinking about them. Although I hope I didn't neglect them, my thoughts were often elsewhere.

These days it's just part of family life that my job sometimes takes me away from them emotionally if not physically.

By now my daughters are used to the fact that I function to some extent independently of them, and I've encouraged them to be independent of me. In practice that means they can cook, iron, and generally take care of themselves.

I've always tried to be fairly firm with them and that has made life easier for all of us, but I enjoy their company too and spend a lot of time listening to their tales of school and discussing issues and problems. Much of this is substitute friendship for me – if I had a partner I would have less time for them. And sometimes their companionship doesn't ease my loneliness because they are too young to act in return as a listening ear for me. When I want to moan about the complexities of work or passion I have to go to friends.

My eldest daughter, now fifteen, has blossomed without her father. His attitude to her had been nervous and belligerent, always telling her off for the slightest thing, and her response was to withdraw to the point of becoming almost unfathomable in her silence. But within a year after his departure, astounded friends reported that she had actually begun to initiate conversations with them. Today she still enjoys her own company but she's much more outgoing and no longer afraid to get involved with people.

Erin found the breakup harder to accept, and more painful. She's nearly twelve now, and I fear that she will look for her dad in every boy she meets. Erin is very people-centred and she made sure that her father paid her plenty of attention. For several years after the breakup she held me responsible for his unhappiness (he used to cry a lot in front of them). Then, as he gradually lost contact, I continued to bolster their confidence by insisting that he still loved them, that he was just very busy, and so on.

One night, when she was about eight or nine, I blew my top and told her what I really thought of her father – that he was childish, selfish and immature, with no sense of parental responsibility whatsoever. The result was amazing.

'But why', asked my little daughter 'didn't you tell me this before?'

She said that knowing those things would have made it so much easier for her to cope when he failed to get in touch. She felt I'd been wrong to give her a false picture, although she understood that I did it to protect her. After that night we have been much closer, and I no longer try to sugar the pill. She's sad about her lost father, but she's also more realistic about the situation as a whole.

They haven't seen him for nearly three years now, and it bothers me that in this all-female household they are no longer used to having men around. They seem to see men as an alien species and are probably quite frightened of them. The only man they've ever lived with was volatile and unpredictable, and that experience must colour their expectations of men in general. It worries me that their future relationships will always be shadowed by the cloud of their father's influence.

In 1988 I graduated from my degree course. The honeymoon was over and it was time to become a proper family bread-winner. I'd got a place on a postgraduate teacher training course, but the very thought of working full time in a school depressed me. Most of my teacher friends were already overworked and disillusioned. On the other hand, the kids had endured four years of poverty while I studied and it seemed only fair that they should look forward to a more prosperous life.

Then, in the summer, events took an unexpected turn. I'd recently begun writing again and was advised to go on a week's course at The Arvon Foundation. The tutors gave me plenty of positive feedback and encouraged me to keep trying.

'If you want to get anywhere, you'd better write a novel,' they said.

Okay. I'd write a novel. I was running short of priorities at the time and that one looked very attractive.

It also seemed to be a possibility. I devised a Grand Plan, the grandest of all so far. Within two months I'd sold the house for a good profit and purchased a much smaller one, half a mile away. We decided to use some of the extra money to insure us against future poverty, and then we went on a crazy spending spree! A better car, new carpets throughout, new furniture and cabin-beds for the kids, a washer-drier, portable TV – you name it. We just spent and spent! In a flash of responsibility I even bought myself a pension to guard against my old age, which seems to be getting nearer by the minute.

I had already been offered some part-time teaching at the Polytechnic, and the idea was that I would supplement those earnings with the rest of the house profits for two years. I swore to myself that if by the end of that time I was not able to support us with writing, then I would definitely get a Proper Job.

It was a crazy and unrealistic idea, but it was a last dash to safety before respectability closed in on me. Surely that mad surge of intellectual activity couldn't just end after four exciting years?

Well, I was lucky. With the help of two writer's bursaries I managed to keep body and soul together long enough to complete *Correspondence*, my first novel. As I write, I've been out of college for nearly three years and have not yet had a Proper Job. The book got itself an agent and was shortlisted for an award even before it was accepted by The Women's Press, and on the strength of it I've found various short-term jobs teaching Creative Writing.

Now I divide my time between writing and teaching. The days are quiet here in our tiny house on the edge of town, and married life seems a million years away.

It is very hard for me to imagine who I was eight years ago. She was a different person, and although her frustrations still sometimes bubble up in my work, I generally think about her very little.

Before my marriage ended I had very little self-confidence. Even though I had actually instigated the breakup, I had been afraid that I wouldn't be able to cope without a partner. Now I look back with astonishment at my dependence on a relationship which had actually depleted that very autonomy and self-confidence.

Sadly, however, many women like me have lost out in other ways, especially romantically. We present a threatening image to men which decimates our chances of ever securing a lasting heterosexual partnership.

We are tough, particular, and self-driven. Having been married to fools, we do not suffer them gladly. Weighed down by responsibilities of children and jobs we have lost our child-like innocence, and it's hard to invite someone to stay for the night when you know the kids will glare balefully at them over the breakfast table.

Who's that, Mum? Not another one! You're not going out again, Mum?

And indeed, why should they suffer strangers who stay overnight and wait embarrassed at the bathroom door in the morning? And is it really worth it for your lover, to make all that effort just to get to know you, just in case you hit it off eventually? No, of course it's not. Courtship with a single parent is damned hard work – for both of you.

I've been without a lover for five years now. Sometimes I get very lonely, and I do miss the thrills and spills of romance, but mostly I'm so excited by my work that I forget to be sad. I'd like to share my life with someone but of course that depends on things out of my control.

There's one more dream I must mention. I only ever had this dream once and always wondered what it was about. It has remained vivid for over twenty years.

I'm standing in a wide foyer. Before me is a glass kiosk and inside it sits a woman. To one side of her curves an enormous staircase and halfway up it stands another woman, pausing to look back as she ascends. She's tall and statuesque and dressed in a gleaming white boilersuit. The strangest thing is the staircase – although it looks like white marble, every step is made of books.

This dream intrigued me for years, but now I think I understand it. I know I have left the glass case and I'm the woman climbing the stairs, towards . . . what? It's my new priority to find out!

PRELUDE

Clare Venables

For a split second, in the bath this morning,
the veil broke and I touched a loving sense
of what life is. Outside a magpie croaked.
For only a moment, the lino (torn), the shampoo
bottles with the tops left off, the Christmas
paper stuck to the wall with Uhu last
July to cover a bald patch, leaking now,
the favourite Warehouse dress hanging on
the back of the old blue door, for only a moment
they shimmer in connection. Seeing them clear
I clearly see the trees outside my study
window, hear the birds as, dripping in my
towel, I scribble down these tiny words.

'Not good enough,' Professor Prior said
in his frail room suspended in the cold
Arts corridor. 'To say "Because I know"
to Bishop Berkeley pondering the state
of the kitchen table's claim on our attention,

118

to say "I KNOW it's there!" does not refute
his basic theory that we cannot know
unless we posit some all-seeing eye.'
Everyone laughed, including me, at my
elated outrage at 'We cannot know.'
Why did I laugh? In laughing I denied
the blood and smell of my own flesh, sensible
to the fragile trembling universe.
'Draw a veil,' my mother kindly said
when, noticing my father's angry face
I piercingly demanded what was wrong.
The veil was drawn across, my childish arrow
lost its mark. A hairline fracture creeping
up my heart wobbled me off course,
and I have wandered baffled ever since.

But the lino (torn) in the bathroom holds my tread,
the blue door meets my hand as I push it open;
here disconnection crumbles to breathing flesh.
Goodbye Professor Prior, goodbye my loving
Ma. I listen to a language now
that weaves among the gravestones of your minds,
leading me smiling through the long and living
grass. Worms and knitting, coffee cups
and mould, bumble bees and tablecloths
hang in the juicy cavities around
my heart. Home. I've landed here by chance
escorted by some lino (torn) and dusty
shampoo bottles with the tops left off.

A RICHER AND MORE VARIED LIFE

Margaret Edmonds

My husband announced his intention to leave me, without any forewarning, when I discovered that he had been having an affair for eighteen months. Forget all those sages who say the wife always knows about a husband's affairs, this one did not. Maybe I was stupid, maybe I was ignoring the signs which, with the wonderful gift of hindsight, I gradually came to see all too clearly. Maybe I subconsciously chose to attribute other reasons to the moods, absent-mindedness, odd comments and slightly out-of-character behaviour. I truly thought that I loved this man and that I trusted him absolutely. We had been married for twenty-two years and had daughters who were twenty-one and eighteen, and on the point of leaving home. Although it had not always been an easy marriage, I had not sensed any reason for thinking that separation was likely. My thoughts were turning to being able to spend more time developing our interests together.

My husband had clearly been thinking on different lines. Tired of what he described as having always to compromise, he was now opting for freedom, independence and shedding of responsibilities. His choice of companion was a girl of twenty-two, one year older than our eldest daughter, nearly half my age and twenty-seven years his junior. Perhaps only another woman of a similar age can really understand how this felt. Not only was this man telling me that what amounted to my life's work was on the rubbish heap, he was consigning me to that same tip. I felt like an old used car being traded in for a new model. I was completely demoralised, my self-confidence wiped out. I was coincidentally made redundant at work. I did not really care much about the job, but coming at this time, it was an additional rejection.

Writing about my feelings at that time is difficult. On paper the words look either trite or melodramatic, and the mind-bending awfulness of the situation becomes banal. I remember that I seemed to experience every kind of negative emotion, which formed a long, painful nightmare of grief, anger, self-pity, outrage and despair. For weeks I cried and slept, slept and cried. Getting up was a pointless effort; bathing and dressing resulted in physical exhaustion. My body felt weak and heavy; I could not eat and I lost over a stone in weight. There were many times I seriously contemplated suicide and I began to drink too much.

The phases of energy I did have were largely channelled into furious anger against my husband. For practical reasons, we did not actually separate for several months and in that time I was able to rid myself of much fury and bitterness. As a result, when I eventually started to reconstruct my life, I was able to do so with less resentment than I might otherwise have had. Although I don't think my husband quite saw it in that light!

It never seriously occurred to me that my husband would change his mind. I do not think I would have wanted him to: I knew the feelings I had for him had changed irrevocably. Acknowledging this forced me to focus on what to do about it. I was damned if I was going to let the actions of one man mess up the rest of my life. I was determined to establish to myself and everyone else that the loss was his and not mine. Of course it wasn't simple getting into that state of mind, and it took time, work, friends, family, my children and now grandchildren to help me construct that alternative. Neither was it a matter of continuous upward progression – it was more like being on the Big Dipper, and sometimes it still is.

I did have a few pluses to help me make my new start. My husband moved right away from the area. Knowing that I was not likely to bump into him and his new partner round every street corner was a great help. Also, I was not completely destitute financially as he had agreed to make over his share of the house to me, in lieu of maintenance payments. I knew that the chances of getting regular payments were slim and I did not want to be dependent on him for any more than I absolutely had to. But the most significant bonus was the studying I had taken up whilst doing the very boring job from which I had been made redundant. Though I did not realise it at the time, this was to be the key to filling many of the physical, mental and emotional spaces with which I had been left.

The most pressing decision I had to make was how to earn a living. I had a varied employment background, and I felt instinctively that I needed to do something more positive, to take the opportunity to change direction and find out what I could really do. I had left school at sixteen with a few 'O' levels and very little idea of what the world was about. It was the norm in those days for female education to be geared towards husband, home and children, and, with the added influence of a Catholic upbringing, it was not long before I and many of my contemporaries were collecting wedding rings and producing babies. Years later, having studied to make myself more employable, I had rediscovered the pleasure of learning. It suddenly occurred to me (while doing the washing-up!) that this might enable me to go to university. The possibility seemed at once so unlikely and yet such a perfect solution that I hardly dared to believe it could be realised. But once I decided to make this my goal it all seemed to happen with extraordinary ease. A friend gave me the kick start I needed

122

to get through the application procedures, my qualifications were accepted and I was eventually offered places at *two* universities.

My daughters were extremely supportive and proud of what I was doing, while friends' reactions ranged from envy, curiosity and disbelief to enthusiasm, congratulations and support. I have to admit that where there was admiration I received it like manna from heaven; admiration was something I had not experienced for a long time and I used it to sustain and motivate myself through many difficult periods.

Altogether, I spent six years at university as an undergraduate and then as a postgraduate student. I had naïvely thought that I would be embarking on this new phase of life as an independent adult with grown-up children and no responsibilities, but the reality was different. Within a month of starting, one daughter had fallen ill with pneumonia and the other had announced her impending marriage. I changed universities, fell foul of the sudden surge of inflation and had to move house to a new part of the country. The older daughter's marriage started to go badly wrong and I found myself giving regular shelter and support to her and eventually to two grandchildren. In addition, my mother died quite unexpectedly. Despite this, and problems with my own health brought on by stress, I somehow managed to complete the work and to make friends, many of whom I still have. At the end of my postgrad course it seemed that, in spite of all my efforts, I might be unemployed once again, but another providential event occurred and I was offered temporary work with my present employers. I stayed on, and now I am lucky enough to have the sort of job I could never have dreamt of eight years ago when the world had seemed to stop and I had wanted to get off.

Looking back over that time I know that I have discovered a great deal about myself. Being assertive on my own behalf always used to invoke feelings of guilt, but I have since learned to stand on my own, and handle situations and achieve things for myself that I never even considered before. Most of all I have confidence in myself, because I have proved to my own satisfaction that I can do a great deal. Getting my degree certificate was probably the most public achievement, but there have been many more personal and private ones.

There is no doubt, however, that I would not have got this far without other people to help and motivate me. In the early days there were people who were prepared just to sit and listen. There were also those who gave me encouragement to start moving on the new path I had chosen. Even those who were negative provided a spur, because I simply wanted to prove them wrong. I didn't feel particularly brave about my actions – after all, I did not think I had a great deal more to lose – but I did want to show that I could think and act constructively. Above all I wanted to prove to myself that it might be worth being alive. I had seriously contemplated suicide, particularly in the first few months when absolutely nothing seemed worth waking up for, and I am still not sure what stopped me from it. A large degree of cowardice I suppose, but primarily it was pride. I wanted my children to have a better rôle model than a suicide. And, while I might have relished the idea that responsibility for my death would be laid at my husband's door, I also knew that this would be admitting defeat.

I have often thought that I displayed very few of the so-called virtues during these bad times, but at least three of the deadly sins came to my rescue – anger, vanity and pride. I used them constructively to help rebuild my life. I still do from time to time but I have also learned to use a few virtues, especially as my understanding of other people's dilemmas is now a great deal deeper. Despite, or perhaps because of, the experiences of my Catholic upbringing, I have no particular religious faith. Instead, I armed myself with little pieces of paper depicting scraps of wisdom from philosophers, poets and writers. I still occasionally find them tucked into books or stuffed into pockets of clothes I haven't recently worn. And I still find them useful reminders.

During the past eight years I have hardly seen my now ex-husband. I divorced him after five years' separation. As far as I was concerned we were as good as divorced from the moment we parted. After five years, the formalities are minimal and the procedure easy, and I was well past the stage when seeing divorce papers come through the letterbox was likely to be traumatic. He married again, to the woman with whom he was having the affair, and I cannot help occasionally dwelling on the irony of the situation: I am the one with the independence and freedom of choice *he* claimed *he* was leaving *me* for. I saw him most recently at our younger daughter's wedding and hardly recognised him. It was difficult to reconcile this person with the man I had married; he was a stranger yet not a stranger. I could not associate him with the intimacy of a husband and yet here we were, brought together in the same room by virtue of having a child in common. This established, without a doubt in my mind, that my life now is far richer and more varied than it ever would have been had we stayed together.

I do not have a partner. This is not a matter of choice, it has just not happened. For a long time after our separation I was not interested in other men and watching one or two friends getting involved on the rebound from failed relationships made me even more cautious. Later I found that all my energies and attention were needed to get through the traumas of university work and family problems; men just didn't figure in the equation. I did have one or two short-term encounters which were important in that they restored my confidence as a woman. They also taught me that I did not much like having relationships based on little more than hopping into bed. Nevertheless, if I stop to think that I might always be on my own, I do sometimes get a bit gloomy; and there are often times when I very much want someone to be there, to share the good and bad of life. But most of life's happenings are unplanned and I fully expect that my life will eventually change again in a way that may or may not include someone else.

I am writing this in my fiftieth year, sitting in my own flat, in comfortable surroundings and with possessions I have purchased by my own efforts. My job is demanding but rewarding, providing both mental stimulation and a very reasonable income. My daughters have married this year (second time around for the eldest), I have two smashing grandchildren and the health and strength to enjoy it all.

If I had written this account at any earlier time, it might have had a different, maybe less optimistic perspective. The point is that this is where I am now, and that it is possible to get here. I do not want to underemphasise the problems and setbacks, nor the times of black depression, and I know that many women are left in far worse circumstances than mine. But gaps do start to appear in the constant blackness of the early days, those gaps eventually get bigger and the black days further apart. They still occur for me, but now I have learned to cope with them and know that they do pass.

To any woman, or man for that matter, now in those awful early days of separation, or finding it hard to come to terms with a new situation, I would say, hold on to the knowledge that life can get better if you want it to. But let go of the past because it can't be recaptured. And *never* allow yourself to think that it must be all your fault. Find something positive to keep aiming for until eventually you will realise that the most positive thing worth living for is yourself.